Unschooling Dads
Twenty-two Testimonials on Their
Unconventional Approach to Education

Edited by Skyler J. Collins
Foreword by Sandra Dodd

Everything-Voluntary.com

Published 2015 by Skyler J. Collins
Visit: www.skylerjcollins.com

Cover design by KindleBookeCovers.com

Licensed under Creative Commons
Attribution 4.0 International

ISBN-13: 978-1517128609
ISBN-10: 1517128609

To the dad who only wants what's best for his child.

CONTENTS

	Foreword – Sandra Dodd	i
	Preface – Skyler J. Collins	vii
1	What is Unschooling? – Earl Stevens	1
2	Prospective Unschooling Dads	11
3	Junior Unschooling Dads	35
4	Senior Unschooling Dads	97
	Epilogue – Phillip Eger	137
	Further Reading	139
	Dad Index	140

FOREWORD

This is a good book. This book has been needed and I'm glad Skyler Collins found and inspired these men to share their thoughts and experiences.

This is an important book. I'm glad you have it and are about to read more. It will help make many children's lives wonderful. When the parents relax enough to see the wonder in their children, then their own lives will improve. As each life is made richer and more peaceful, the family grows lighter, and happier.

Unschooling sounds crazy. Peeking out of school doorways, or out of school eyes, it looks dangerously insane. But here's the deal: school-eyes come of having lived in school, identified with school, having become schooled, and schoolish. Peeking out of a school doorway is no place to stand to see the whole real world.

This book lets you see from different continents and from the perspectives of dads from different decades, whose children are all different ages. They have gone on the dangerous, scary path, and have left messages here for you to come on—it's a pretty nice path after all.

Don't be surprised if reading this causes you to alternate between attraction and aversion. That's normal and healthy, but don't believe everything you think. There are some voices in your head that you might want to say "Enough" to now, for the benefit of your inner child, your living outer children, and your own future ability to think freely and widely.

Over twenty years of communicating with unschoolers, I have only counted a dozen men who discovered and desired unschooling before their wives did. Thousands of moms, a dozen dads. Skyler Collins was one of that dozen. Those represented in this book are about half and half. Be glad if you're one of those dads who gets to be persuasive rather than defensive. And if you're being persuaded by someone excited about unschooling, I hope this book will help you see different facets and possibilities from a male stance.

For years when moms asked what might convince a dad who didn't want to read, who thought things were fine and school was great, unschoolers would say "Get him to a conference where he can see unschooling dads interacting with their children." That has helped many, but there are dads who won't go, or who can't go because they're musicians, chefs, emergency room doctors and the weekends are their main work days. There are families for whom conferences are too far away or too great an expense. The stories in this book might give you some of that benefit, though you'll miss the joy of the eyes lighting up between a joyous child and a dad who knows he is contributing to that joy. If you can find more experienced families to meet and hang out with, somehow, there can be value in seeing those relationships.

Sometimes dads are impressed by seeing older kids—tweens, teens—especially if they're familiar with any currently schooled kids of the same ages. A dad I know coaches girls' soccer. His confidence in his own daughters grew as he dealt with so many others their age. Some unschooling dads are teachers, or public servants dealing with children, and they too have reported a growing appreciation for benefits their children have gained from an unpressured life filled with real choices.

My husband, Keith Dodd, didn't write for this book, but he has spoken at conferences, in groups—a family panel once, and two or three panels of dads. I have saved one thing he said because it stunned me:

"We wanted our children to become thoughtful, intelligent, undamaged adults."

In so short a summary of what we hoped to accomplish by unschooling, he used the word "undamaged." That's quite powerful.

I remind moms, when they're confused about why fathers are "being difficult" about children, that inside every man is the little boy. Women forget that sometimes. When men are energetic, efficient, organized, resourceful and strong it can be easy for women to pour all their gentle nurturing energy onto the children, forgetting that the dad might be needy, too. In varying degrees, childhood hurts can hinder clarity. Sometimes dads are jealous of their children's options and opportunities. Don't banish the little boy inside you, or ignore him. You can nurture and soothe your own soul and psyche by giving your child what you wish you had had when you were that age.

Generosity makes you generous. Kindness makes you kind. Respecting others, and their ideas and their interests, makes you full of respect—respectful. These are little things that build up quickly.

Practicing on children can make it easier to be kind and patient with a spouse, partner or co-parent. Many marriages have improved because of changing attitudes and abilities that grew out of unschooling principles and practices. And just as surviving a disaster, pulling through an emergency, or remodeling a house can bring a couple together with shared memories, pride and mutual admiration (or relief that it's over), so can looking back at successful parenting experiences. When things go well and both parents contributed to that, it strengthens the partnership. That was an unexpected benefit of unschooling, but it's not a fluke.

This book can soothe and support, inspire and uplift. Relax. Allow your thoughts and hopes to rise. It's easy to "Yeah but" and "What if" yourself into a hole; don't. You'll pull your family into the hole with you.

If you move into unschooling, you won't become a fantasy dad. You will still be you. Your children will be the humans they were born to be, but perhaps you can assist in helping them grow up undamaged. With practice, you can find ways to nurture a relationship with each child that could improve generations of your family to come.

Those who read here will be doing a good thing. Those who wrote at Skyler's request have done a great thing. Channel these positives into your children's lives, and may you have many years of peace together.

- Sandra Dodd, Senior Unschooling Mom

PREFACE

I was the mover and shaker in my family regarding unschooling. This is not a very common thing, as noted in the preceding Foreword by long-time unschooling mom Sandra Dodd. My own experience bouncing among support groups mirrors hers, "Thousands of moms, a dozen dads."

I have brought together in this book nearly two dozen dads or future dads who have written their personal accounts on why and how they chose unschooling for their children. What's remarkable is the type of men here represented. We have entrepreneurs and business professionals, but also college professors, artists, world travelers, and computer experts. These are intelligent and thoughtful men, a few of whom are heavily involved in academia. That's very telling to me. Unschooling is not a backward or crazy idea, though it certainly *seems* that way at first. It has attracted and proven itself to incredibly smart individuals, both moms and dads. Sandra Dodd herself majored in English with minors in psychology and anthropology.

This book begins with an introduction to unschooling by senior unschooling dad Earl Stevens. After which it contains three chapters written by dads or future dads at different periods in their unschooling journey. It ends with a somewhat humorous epilogue written by junior unschooling dad (and my good friend) Phillip Eger.

If what you've read has intrigued you, then take some time to discover the *hows* of unschooling via the Further Reading page at the end. Those books, sites, and even a podcast archive do a fantastic job explaining unschooling through the experiences of real unschoolers. If at any point you have questions about unschooling, feel free to contact anyone in this book. Links to their Facebook profiles are included at the end of their testimonials.

Acknowledgements

I want to thank all of those who contributed to this book. Your efforts made this possible. I also want to thank Sandra Dodd for everything she has done for the unschooling community. Her website, SandraDodd.com, has been an invaluable resource to me over the last few years, and will no doubt continue to be invaluable in the future. Finally, I want to thank my beautiful and benevolent wife, Julieta, for bearing me three (so far) wonderful and wonder-filled children, and for being both skeptical and acquiescent as we headed into the unknown.

- Skyler Collins, Editor

1 WHAT IS UNSCHOOLING?

"What we want to see is the child in pursuit of knowledge, not knowledge in pursuit of the child."
– George Bernard Shaw

It is very satisfying for parents to see their children in pursuit of knowledge. It is natural and healthy for the children, and in the first few years of life, the pursuit goes on during every waking hour. But after a few short years, most kids go to school. The schools also want to see children in pursuit of knowledge, but the schools want them to pursue mainly the school's knowledge and devote twelve years of life to doing so.

In his acceptance speech for the New York City Teacher of the Year award (1990), John Gatto said,

"Schools were designed by Horace Mann... and others to be instruments of the scientific management of a mass population." In the interests of managing each generation of children, the public school curriculum has become a hopelessly flawed attempt to define education and to find a way of delivering that definition to vast numbers of children.

The traditional curriculum is based on the assumption that children must be pursued by knowledge because they will never pursue it themselves. It was no doubt noticed that, when given a choice, most children prefer not to do school work. Since, in a school, knowledge is defined as schoolwork, it is easy for educators to conclude that children don't like to acquire knowledge. Thus schooling came to be a method of controlling children and forcing them to do whatever educators decided was beneficial for them. Most children don't like textbooks, workbooks, quizzes, rote memorization, subject schedules, and lengthy periods of physical inactivity. One can discover this—even with polite and cooperative children—by asking them if they would like to add more time to their daily schedule. I feel certain that most will decline the offer.

ON THEIR UNCONVENTIONAL APPROACH TO EDUCATION

The work of a schoolteacher is not the same as that of a homeschooling parent. In most schools, a teacher is hired to deliver a ready-made, standardized, year-long curriculum to 25 or more age-segregated children who are confined in a building all day. The teacher must use a standard curriculum—not because it is the best approach for encouraging an individual child to learn the things that need to be known—but because it is a convenient way to handle and track large numbers of children. The school curriculum is understandable only in the context of bringing administrative order out of daily chaos, of giving direction to frustrated children and unpredictable teachers. It is a system that staggers ever onward but never upward, and every morning we read about the results in our newspapers.

But despite the differences between the school environment and the home, many parents begin homeschooling under the impression that it can be pursued only by following some variation of the traditional public school curriculum in the home. Preoccupied with the idea of "equivalent education", state and local education officials assume that we must share their educational goals and that we homeschool simply because we don't want our children to be inside their buildings.

Textbook and curriculum publishing companies go to great lengths to assure us that we must buy their products if we expect our children to be properly educated. As if this were not enough, there are national, state, and local support organizations that have practically adopted the use of the traditional curriculum and the school-in-the-home image of homeschooling as a de facto membership requirement. In the midst of all this, it can be difficult for a new home-schooling family to think that an alternative approach is possible.

One alternative approach is "unschooling," also known as "life learning," "experience-based learning," or "independent learning." Several weeks ago, when our homeschooling support group announced a gathering to discuss unschooling, we thought a dozen or so people might attend, but more than 100 adults and children showed up. For three hours, parents and some of the children took turns talking about their homeschooling experiences and about unschooling. Many people said afterward that they left the meeting feeling reinforced and exhilarated—not because anybody told them what to do or gave them a magic formula—but because they grew more secure in making these decisions for themselves. Sharing ideas about this topic left them feeling empowered.

Before I talk about what I think unschooling is, I must talk about what it isn't. Unschooling isn't a recipe, and therefore it can't be explained in recipe terms. It is impossible to give unschooling directions for people to follow so that it can be tried for a week or so to see if it works. Unschooling isn't a method, it is a way of looking at children and at life. It is based on trust that parents and children will find the paths that work best for them—without depending on educational institutions, publishing companies, or experts to tell them what to do.

Unschooling does not mean that parents can never teach anything to their children, or that children should learn about life entirely on their own without the help and guidance of their parents. Unschooling does not mean that parents give up active participation in the education and development of their children and simply hope that something good will happen. Finally, since many unschooling families have definite plans for college, unschooling does not even mean that children will never take a course in any kind of a school.

Then what is unschooling? I can't speak for every person who uses the term, but I can talk about my own experiences. Our son has never had an academic lesson, has never been told to read or to learn mathematics, science, or history. Nobody has told him about phonics. He has never taken a test or been asked to study or memorize anything. When people ask, "What do you do?" My answer is that we follow our interests—and our interests inevitably lead to science, literature, history, mathematics, music—all the things that have interested people before anybody thought of them as "subjects."

A large component of unschooling is grounded in doing real things, not because we hope they will be good for us, but because they are intrinsically fascinating. There is an energy that comes from this that you can't buy with a curriculum. Children do real things all day long, and in a trusting and supportive home environment, "doing real things" invariably brings about healthy mental development and valuable knowledge. It is natural for children to read, write, play with numbers, learn about society, find out about the past, think, wonder and do all those things that society so unsuccessfully attempts to force upon them in the context of schooling.

While few of us get out of bed in the morning in the mood for a "learning experience," I hope that all of us get up feeling in the mood for life. Children always do so—unless they are ill or life has been made overly stressful or confusing for them. Sometimes the problem for the parent is that it can be difficult to determine if anything important is actually going on. It is a little like watching a garden grow. No matter how closely we examine the garden, it is difficult to verify that anything is happening at that particular moment. But as the season progresses, we can see that much has happened, quietly and naturally. Children pursue life, and in doing so, pursue knowledge. They need adults to trust in the inevitability of this very natural process, and to offer what assistance they can.

Parents come to our unschooling discussions with many questions about fulfilling state requirements. They ask: "How do unschoolers explain themselves to the state when they fill out the paperwork every year?", "If you don't use a curriculum, what do you say?" and "What about required record-keeping?" To my knowledge, unschoolers have had no problems with their state departments of education over matters of this kind. This is a time when even many public school educators are moving away from the traditional curriculum, and are seeking alternatives to fragmented learning and drudgery.

When I fill out the paperwork required for homeschooling in our state, I briefly describe, in the space provided, what we are currently doing, and the general intent of what we plan to do for the coming year. I don't include long lists of books or describe any of the step-by-step skills associated with a curriculum. For example, under English/Language Arts, I mentioned that our son's favorite "subject" is the English language. I said a few words about our family library. I mentioned that our son reads a great deal and uses our computer for whatever writing he happens to do. I concluded that, "Since he already does so well on his own, we have decided not to introduce language skills as a subject to be studied. It seems to make more sense for us to leave him to his own continuing success."

Unschooling is a unique opportunity for each family to do whatever makes sense for the growth and development of their children. If we have a reason for using a curriculum and traditional school materials, we are free to use them. They are not a universally necessary or required component of unschooling, either educationally or legally.

Allowing curriculums, textbooks, and tests to be the defining, driving force behind the education of a child is a hindrance in the home as much as in the school—not only because it interferes with learning, but because it interferes with trust. As I have mentioned, even educators are beginning to question the pre-planned, year-long curriculum as an outdated, 19th-century educational system. There is no reason that families should be less flexible and innovative than schools.

Anne Sullivan, Helen Keller's mentor and friend, said:

> "I am beginning to suspect all elaborate and special systems of education. They seem to me to be built upon the supposition that every child is a kind of idiot who must be taught to think. Whereas if the child is left to himself, he will think more and better, if less 'showily.' Let him come and go freely, let him touch real things and combine his impressions for himself... Teaching fills the mind with artificial associations that must be got rid of before the child can develop independent ideas out of actual experiences."

Unschooling provides a unique opportunity to step away from systems and methods, and to develop independent ideas out of actual experiences, where the child is truly in pursuit of knowledge, not the other way around.

- Earl Stevens, Senior Unschooling Dad (1994)

2 PROSPECTIVE UNSCHOOLING DADS

Chris Moody
Homemaker, Utah, USA

I grew up in a suburb of Seattle, WA called Federal Way and lived there until I left for college at the University of Utah. While studying there I met my wife, Marianne, and we now live in Layton, UT with our 2 children, Camden, 5, and Cleo, 2.

Growing up I attended government schools with no real idea that anything else existed. I had a vague idea that some kids went to private schools, probably from movies, and knew that they were expensive. I don't recall understanding that some kids were homeschooled until I was probably in college. I believed all the myths about homeschool kids (socially inept, limited by parents' knowledge, generally weird and overly nerdy) without ever even looking into the research. I received my degree in Exercise Science about a year after my wife and I were married. I was offered a teaching position at a charter school in Ogden where my wife's cousin was the director (probably a little nepotism).

Teaching P.E. and Health to seventh and eighth graders was an especially interesting time. For me, the only good part of seventh and eighth grade was making friends. I hated many teachers, thought homework was a waste of my time, felt pressure to conform, and learned very little. My parents both worked my entire life and seemed to always be worrying about money, so the idea that school could be something else never crossed their minds. They knew I didn't like school but were probably just happy I never got into any real trouble.

While I was teaching we were required to administer standardized tests and make sure the kids stayed quiet for many hours. I was assigned to a group of eighth graders with a colleague of mine. As we stood around, he showed me a book he had brought and was reading during the testing. The book was *Weapons of Mass Instruction* by John

Taylor Gatto.[1] If you've never read anything by Gatto, know that he taught in public schools for many years (30+, I believe) and was a fierce critic of the compulsory education model. The book resonated with me so deeply. It was as though someone watched a detailed video of my schooling experience and explained why I felt so frustrated, undervalued, and derided. Then it was as if they looked into the future and saw why I consistently underachieved, never even coming close to realizing my potential. It's hard to put into words what effect reading that book had on me.

The simple spark truly changed my life. I read books and articles about unschooling, Sudbury-model schools, lifelong learning, and so forth, with newfound interest and vigor. I even tried to apply the lessons I was learning into my classroom, with fascinating results. It led me to looking into alternatives to almost everything in my life because school was such an institution in my world, one that I had never questioned before.

One aspect of unschooling that stood out most to me was the idea that life is learning. You don't really start or stop learning. You just decide where to put in the effort, even if it seems like you're not

---

[1] Available in several formats at http://skyler.link/amznmassintruct

doing anything. That freedom has really only been available to me since I left the university and I've loved it. I haven't always focused my attention on the best learning I could receive but I am now fully aware that it is my own choice, which all by itself motivates me to seek the best I can.

This style of education would have suited me so completely that I sometimes can't imagine my children doing anything different. That event occurred about 5 years ago and I've learned to not let my enthusiasm for something overrule my better judgment or rational thought processes. My wife, in contrast, loved school. She loved the external motivators and didn't feel pressured in the same ways I did. My son would start kindergarten this fall (2015) and I do have some reservations about unschooling. Though I don't believe the ideas about kids needing public education for social reasons, my son doesn't have many friends in the area. Just to meet other kids I want to send him to the local school. I loved meeting people at school so it seems easier to send him there.

Honestly, outside of that, I have no other fears about unschooling. For me, one of the most powerful things I've learned is that options exist. Maybe my children will go to school all through high school. Maybe they'll love it. Maybe they'll hate it. But I want them to be aware of the options available to them.

Chris Moody is a Seattle-born stay-at-home dad hoping to pass on a fuller life to his two children, Camden and Cleo. He is an obsessive fitness enthusiast who enjoys bouldering, gymnastics, weightlifting, mixed-martial arts and several team sports. He enjoys spending time outdoors with his family whenever possible. You can often find him working on handstands at the park or reading about snakes to his kids. He can be found online at Facebook.com/moody253.

Gregory Diehl
Entrepreneur, Kuala Lumpur, Malaysia

It's nearing my 27th birthday. I am still ostensibly very young and just beginning my journey into adulthood. Yet, I feel as though I have already lived many mini-lives in a rapid period of time.

Since 18, I've tried to learn as much as I could about the way our world rears children. I had to prepare for the day when my kids would rely on me as their creator, caretaker, and teacher about the world around them. To this end, I put myself into positions where I could observe the parenting and teaching styles of as many cultures as possible, each with their own flaws, values, and objectives. Being reared in public school in California, I burned with curiosity to know of a better way to pass on information to future generations. The global unwillingness to treat children as individuals saddens me deeply. I could not accept that this was the best way we've figured out how to interact with our children.

I used teaching and private mentoring experiences to learn from the parenting mistakes of others. I made it my mission to practice the skill of parenting on pseudo-siblings and faux-offspring in every chance I could get. I observed that every family unit carries its own narrative on what parenting is supposed to be, and what a successful child looks like. These narratives go on to shape almost everything about how a child sees himself and the world throughout his life.

Travel brought me to the inner workings of government schools in China–monolithic empires where children spend 14 hours a day being bred into subservience. Later, I came to live with a

Chinese family as a tutor for their young children, which gave me rare insight into the struggles of a family that sought to break out of the constraints of their culture.

In the Kurdish region of Iraq, I saw how the wealthy could send their children to private schools which overwhelmed them with as much information as possible and achieving high test scores on quarterly assessments. Automatic firearms guarded every entrance, and school buses were checked for hidden explosives daily. Still, the gears of the machine kept turning.

At an Italian Montessori preschool, infants and toddlers were given more chances to play outside and experiment with artistic output. Their time every day still fell into a strict pattern of acceptable activities, and rarely were they allowed to truly explore the depths of their creativity on their own terms.

In my mind, the role of a father is to give his children the physical, intellectual, and emotional tools they will need to live in the world. Beyond basic survival skills, they should be empowered to forge a path unique to their own passions. The good parent walks a fine line between watching over them, without actively inhibiting their exploration of the world. It means encouraging their curiosity without controlling it.

Our children should be able to look up to us as living examples of what they are capable of–not as enforcers of rules and limitations. Though my childhood influences linger on my subconscious to this day, I know I am not forced to repeat the same patterns my parents and culture instilled onto me.

This is a fear which pervades the minds of many future and recent parents. Because we don't believe in our own abilities to teach our kids how the world works, we outsource the most important parts of our children's upbringing to institutions which hold no accountability for ignoring the unique needs of every child. We must believe in ourselves first before we can shape a future for our children.

To be the father my future children deserve, I must pursue the same boundless self-expansion I wish for them. This means challenging myself to always learn more and take on difficult tasks. It means remembering to look at unfamiliar things with childlike enthusiasm (as an aside: if you ever need to be reminded of what pure unbridled curiosity looks like, spend more time with cats; be like the cat).

It is my responsibility to foster an environment where they will receive abundant access to the support that makes their success possible. This kind of influence is what modern schools attempt to provide by shuffling our kids through many teachers and immersing them in a sea of unsegregated peers. They randomize social Influence, and remove all parental discretion from the process. I made it my mission to find the places on earth where I can affect the social influences which will shape children as they break out into the world around them.

Many older parents unconsciously feel threatened by their children's vitality. To them, it is a reminder of the youth they've lost. I will make it my mission to meet my children where they live—to eagerly jump into strange new worlds and figure challenges out one piece at a time. I have to know I am adaptable enough to adjust to whatever they can throw at me, and change my own actions to give them everything they need.

Schooling as we know it as a product of a society that expects individuals to change to fit its traditions. I want my children to be among the first of a new generation which boldly attempts to remake the world in their image—to expect obsolete designs to adapt to them and not the other way around. But I can only make that happen if I am there during the most crucial moments of their development—and always pushing myself to grow as a father at a rate which exceeds their expanding identities.

Gregory V. Diehl is a business and personal narrative consultant who has traveled the world seeking to understand the way we raise our children and forge our own identities in life. He is working to create his own personal paradise on a gorgeous piece of property in the valley of longevity, Vilcabamba, Ecuador, where he hopes to raise a family on his own terms and at peace with the controlling influences of the world. He can be found online at Facebook.com/gregoryvdiehl.

Jeremy Henggeler
Entrepreneur, New York, USA

My name is Jeremy and I am the father of four year old twin girls. My wife and I are still contemplating whether or not we should add to our brood, but for now our two little ones keep us plenty busy. While my wife is doing the stay-at-home mom thing, I am in and out running my pet-sitting company. It's the kind of work that I end up bringing home, as we board dogs in our house, and that allows me much more time with my girls than your typical working dad receives. In my spare time I co-host a weekly podcast, have been learning audio/video editing to help out with our burgeoning podcasting network, and enjoy doing hands on projects with my kids. I also try to find time to continue my studies in the fields of history, economics, and philosophy.

I was raised by two public school educators and spent much of my young life thinking that I would follow in their footsteps. By the time I reached high school, though, that thought started to change. I was always considered a good student, with excellent grades and a relatively high IQ, but the longer I stayed in school the more bored I became. It wasn't until years later that I finally put the pieces together, but on some level I realized that all I needed to do was memorize certain information and I could ace every test. That realization was the beginning of the end for my trust in the public school system. The further away I got from school, the more I realized that I had been woefully underprepared for life. At first I believed that this was due to me not applying myself to the fullest, but I later came to realize that this was by design. When I reached my thirties, I started to re-learn history and became aware of the Prussian schooling model that had been put in place over 100 years ago.[2] That's when everything started to make sense. I now understood why real economics, actual history, philosophy, and logic (outside the field of mathematics) were not featured in the curriculum: having access to this knowledge can circumvent the obedient citizen endgame that the Prussian system sought to accomplish. It was at that point that I vowed should I ever have children, that they would not be subjected to the public education model.

When I first met my wife, she had been in the special education field for quite some time. I was both surprised and pleased, however, when we began to discuss the possibility of having children and she informed me that she would be in favor of home-based education. She explained that she had her doubts about the education system after being on the inside for so many years and that she also had friends whose kids were thriving in a

---

[2] Read *Education: Free & Compulsory* by Murray Rothbard; available in several formats at http://skyler.link/amzneducation

homeschooling environment. When we found out that my wife was pregnant, we both committed to the idea of keeping our future children out of public school. After our twins were born and started to grow, we began investigating different curriculums and making connections with other parents that were already involved in homeschooling situations. We received a lot of excellent feedback and were certain that we were making the correct decision by following this path. Being given the blessing of my parents, the aforementioned former public school teachers, was an added boost of support that, as I have come to realize, is often lacking in other homeschooling families' so-called support systems. We continued to do our research but assumed that it would only be a matter of settling on a particular curriculum once our girls became of age. It was around that time that a new wrinkle was added: I heard a woman named Dayna Martin being interviewed about being an unschooling mother.

I first became aware of Dayna when she was on Jeff Berwick's podcast. I had heard mentions of the idea of unschooling, but mostly just in passing. My initial reaction was that it seemed like lazy parenting, so I didn't bother to pursue the idea any further. While I rejected the notion of public schooling, the thought of no structure whatsoever seemed like a recipe for disaster. After hearing that interview, though, I began to wonder if I had dismissed the idea of unschooling too quickly. I decided it was time to take a deeper look and I soon realized my original error. I had made the same mistake that so many others had done and continue to do; I assumed unschooling equated to virtually no learning and zero guidance. I hadn't even bothered to consider the positives that such a situation had to offer before dismissing the idea based only on the perceived negatives. With a renewed sense of interest and a more open mind, I began to research the concept of unschooling more honestly than I had done in the past. What I came to realize is that my initial reaction could not have been more wrong.

Once I actually began to take a serious look at what unschooling had to offer, it did not take me long to change my original position. Where I had thought it was a form of lazy parenting, I realized that it was just giving a child more options. Where I had thought it meant a very 'hands off' approach, I found that parents still played a vital role. This wasn't about letting kids do whatever they wanted, it was more about letting them choose what topics interested them. I found that I would still need to help them with the basics like reading, writing and arithmetic, which my wife and I had already started to do around the age of three, but then it would become my job to be their support system. I could guide them when needed, give them ideas to get the ball rolling, and be there for them if and when they became stuck. This was the answer I had been seeking; a way to break free of the cookie cutter, one-size-fits-all mentality of the so-called public school system. By giving kids the option to choose what subjects interested them, or by finding ways to implement their outside interests into learning experiences, they were given the opportunity to expand their horizons and learn at an even faster pace than I had been allowed to by being stuck in a rigid system. They could replace the litany of useless knowledge thrust upon them by standardization passed off as education with real world knowledge, and start gaining actionable skills years before it was considered to be socially acceptable as the "right time." This was the ultimate opportunity for kids to be able to reach their full potential!

I was sold. This was the path I had been in search of and I stumbled upon it at just the right time. Not only will my kids not be forced to sit and recite useless information for years on end, they will also be able to start formulating a life plan years before their contemporaries. Many of the unschooling kids I have come across already have even started their own businesses before the age of sixteen. Not only are these children well-mannered, well-socialized and well-spoken but they also possess a drive not often seen from kids that are grinding their way through 15,000+ hours of the one-size-fits-all monotony that passes for education in public schools. Many of these same kids, the ones who decide that they would like to go on to college, are starting their junior year of college at eighteen and are head and shoulders above their classmates in a myriad of ways. The choice of, well, *choice* has opened doors for them that many kids never even knew existed until much later in life. That is what I want for my kids. I want them to live their lives as they see fit, to take whatever path they see as bringing them the most long term success and happiness. Unschooling will give them every opportunity to achieve just that. This is not to say that kids in other situations do not possess the same capabilities, but rather that those kids are given extra roadblocks that I refuse to put in front of my own. My job is to help guide them, not hinder their performance. That is why unschooling makes the most sense to me. As I started off this piece by saying, my girls are only just turning four as I write these words. My wife and I may start with a hybrid of homeschooling and unschooling to get the ball rolling. That may be yet written in stone but we both know what our preferred endgame looks like: our kids engaged in purely self-directed learning and making our own educations literally look like child's play. I honestly can't wait for them to start showing up dear old dad.

Jeremy Henggeler is an entrepreneur who owns and operates a pet-sitting company. He can be found online at Facebook.com/anarchoabolitionist.

Parrish Miller
Web Designer, Idaho, USA

I am a 30-year-old white male living in Idaho. I'm a web designer and social media specialist. I have also worked as a policy analyst, digital media manager, blogger, and journalist at various points in my life. I have always had a keen interest in history, government, and economics; and I have been very involved in politics and the political process since 2008. Today, I actually find philosophy more interesting than politics and am focused particularly on alternative ideas such as counter-economics, the sharing economy, agorism, voluntaryism, and unschooling.

Although I was educated at home, it was far from unschooling. I was enrolled in a formalized correspondence-style education which was formatted on a private, religious school. While it is not exactly what I would have preferred in retrospect, I believe it was far superior to a traditional public or private education. I had more leeway regarding scheduling and I was free from the bullying and peer pressure that are so endemic to both public and private schools.

My education was not confined to what I learned in the school portion of my day, fortunately. I read hundreds of books ranging from kid's novels to scholarly books on history and economics. I borrowed countless items from my local library and enjoyed copying schematics and plans onto graph paper just for fun. I never felt much kinship with people my own age. Even as a young child, I preferred the company of adults. Children were boring to me and never wanted to talk about things that mattered.

Contrary to the hand-wringing of naysayers, I was never 'socially awkward' or otherwise unprepared for life in the real world. If anything, I was more prepared than many of my peers. Having not wasted the first two decades of my life learning how to interact with children, I was comfortable interacting with educated adults and discussing matters of Importance. I never felt like I missed anything being educated at home, and to this day I am thankful I was not thrown into the lion's den of public education.

Today I would classify myself as a lifelong student, but happily not a professional one. I don't particularly enjoy formalized education even as an adult, and I find sitting in an uncomfortable chair and listening to a lecturer drone on about a topic for which even he can't muster up any enthusiasm a colossal waste of time. To me, real education is not about teachers and students, but about the process of learning. I don't need to be in a classroom or lecture hall to obtain knowledge, and I don't need a PhD in order to impart knowledge to others.

Formalized education (be it Kindergarten or a Master's Seminar) is far too rigid for my liking. I don't want the pre-packaged bits of knowledge which someone else has determined to be the 'right' information for me to have. I don't want to be told what I 'should' know on a subject. There is no universal bucket of knowledge which everyone must possess. Some incredibly intelligent people misspell common words while others with impeccable grammar can't fathom even basic economic concepts. The classical idea of a "Renaissance man" who is knowledgeable in many fields is an interesting concept to aspire to, but it is an increasingly unreachable goal as both the quantity of fields and the knowledge within these fields expand exponentially. No one can know everything, and once that fact is accepted, the idea that self-appointed experts should determine what anyone should know becomes even more preposterous.

I don't have any children right now although I expect that I will have at least one at some point in my life. While I don't want to create any rigid absolutes for how I will raise her—I want to be open to all possibilities and adapt to her personality—if there is one thing I can say with at least 99 percent confidence, it is that I don't want to send her to a traditional school. My reasons for this decision are numerous, but the most important is simply that I want to give my child the opportunity to be a unique individual with as much freedom and choice as possible.

When I first heard the word 'unschooling' several years ago, I assumed it meant the process of un-learning all the misinformation one tends to be taught in school. I soon learned that my supposition was incorrect and that it actually referred to a concept of education that rejected the rigidity of traditional schooling and instead focused on allowing students to choose their own path. I was enamored with the concept immediately as it combined two things I very much support—home-based education and personal choice.

In the modern, information age, I believe that education should not be focused on rote memorization and teaching to the test. If I need to know what year Columbus discovered America, I can ask Google—and hopefully come to realize that Columbus was 500 years late in 'discovering' America, never actually reached America, and was a horrible slave trader as well. Real education is about learning how to learn, not memorizing trivia. I'm okay if my child doesn't remember all the historical dates which were drilled into my head so long as she knows why history matters and how to look up the dates when she needs them. I'm okay if my child never wins a spelling bee so long as she can articulate her thoughts without struggling due to limited language skills. I'm okay if my child can't do long division in her head so long as she can understand that borrowing a million dollars a minute when you're already 18 trillion in debt is unsustainable. And who knows? She may learn all of the above and much more simply because she wants to and no one is telling her she has to. I'm okay with that outcome as well.

I can understand why some people are skeptical about letting their children direct their own education. Many parents have a tendency to be control freaks and want to micromanage every aspect of their child's existence in the hopes that harm can be minimized and opportunity maximized, but the irony is that those parents often have the most screwed up kids of all. I don't believe that healthy, well-adjusted people are the product of centralized planning. It doesn't work for nations (which is why Communism always fails) and it doesn't work for families.

An unschooled child may not think and act exactly like her peers. She may not learn the same things in the same years and thus may not ace standardized tests. She may know a lot about some things which interest her and very little about others which do not. These aren't defects in the theory of unschooling, they are the point! Giving people freedom may be unpredictable, but that doesn't mean it's dangerous. Personally, I look forward to seeing what my child will choose to learn and what will interest her. I will happily use those things to help her think about subjects like math and grammar rather than using stale books and boring word problems.

Traditional education is extremely authoritarian in nature. It affords little room for those who think differently or who deviate from the "the index card of allowable opinion" as Tom Woods likes to say. It is a system built on conformity and tradition which has little to no patience with those who refuse to fall in line. Such a system is one I wouldn't wish on my worst enemy. I can't imagine willingly putting my child into a box like that.

If you believe in liberty, spontaneous order, and peaceful parenting, then unschooling should be right up your alley. It takes the most fundamental principles of a free society and applies them to one of the most formative periods of a child's life. It allows a child to become and to be their own person and to pursue goals and interests based on choice rather than coercion. To me, it's the obvious answer to one of life's greatest questions: How do I give my children a better world than I inherited? What better way than to give them the freedom to be unique individuals who can learn and grow and thrive in a world that isn't built to control them, but to aid them in their pursuit of happiness. That's the world I want to give my children. That's the reason why I choose unschooling.

Parrish Miller is a web designer and social media specialist. He can be found online at Facebook.com/parrishmiller.

3 JUNIOR UNSCHOOLING DADS

Alan Southgate
Musician, Norwich, UK

I'm a musician and music tutor from the UK. I have three daughters, the eldest of which—from a previous relationship—is in public school, the younger two are homeschooled; they are twelve, seven and five, respectively. In recent years I have developed a passion for the 'philosophy of liberty'; this increasingly informs every aspect of my life; from learning to integrate, heal and minimise the influence of emotional wounds received in my past, to finding ways of achieving financial freedom, as well as raising my children in a way that supports their burgeoning autonomy and self-ownership.

My partner and I are attempting to share childcare as much as possible. We are both self-employed and are developing businesses that aim to support our lifestyle, which centres on homeschooling our younger two children. We tend to spend weekends together as a family but during the week I'm solely responsible for the children for three days; at the moment this involves a lot of child-led play, reading aloud, days out with other home-ed families and lengthy conversations centred on conflict resolution!

In all honesty the challenges I face are much more to do with me than the children themselves, ways in which my actions contradict my principles, for example. I'm trying to do away with arbitrary authority in my fathering but having been raised in a 'traditional' environment of punishment, reward and provisional self-esteem, I find myself triggered during day-to-day moments with the children; this is happening less and less the more I grow as a parent and 'when all is well with Dad, all is well with the children' appears to be the rule.

The only real obstacle we have faced—aside from some unfounded concern about our efficacy as educators—is an economic one; it is extremely difficult for one parent to earn a living wage that will support a stay-at-home parent and children. My partner and I are both working hard to develop businesses that will afford us enough money and time to continue to home-educate. Currently it's a struggle to offer as much opportunity and resources as we would like, though we overcome this with some creative thinking and sheer will and determination!

As the children progress I'm delighted to get feedback about them from other adults; I often receive compliments that my two daughters are intelligent, articulate and that they are fiercely independent thinkers. One criticism I have often heard is that home-educated children lack social skills and find integration with 'schooled' children somewhat difficult; I have found the opposite to be the case; both of mine will fearlessly address anyone of any age in a way that I think my eldest daughter had schooled out of her. Another quite unexpected but very welcome benefit to being a home-educating dad is the opportunity—or more appropriately—the necessity for personal growth in order to meet the challenge; I understand that this might be a daunting prospect for some, but I have found it richly rewarding. If I were to have outsourced responsibility for my children's education to a school, I think my character would not have developed as it now has. In order to meet my children's needs, I've needed to look hard at how my needs weren't met as a child and the impact that that has had on my life; in order to nurture self-esteem, I've had to repair and build my own—hard, but immeasurably valuable, work!

The greatest anxiety I have going forward is again related to my role: "What if I haven't got what it takes? What if I'm undermining my children's future?" This comes up a lot but if I reason it out with my partner I generally find reassurance. There's also the pressure of the economic situation in the UK; it's very difficult to maintain the home-ed lifestyle when wages are so low relative to the cost of living. If my partner and I cannot earn enough between us then we may be forced to send the children to school; I'm uncertain as to how I would deal with that, if it comes up.

We try to be peaceful parents, I certainly try to be principled in my approach to discipline. One of the real advantages of home-ed is that you can take the time to talk things through if there is a problem that requires intervention; I try to examine each occurrence logically with the children, taking individual needs into account, and I encourage the children to help resolve any issues.

Most importantly, I try to be clear about the principles at work behind my fathering—non-aggression and property rights being the main two. One consequence of this is that my daughters will call me out on my inconsistencies! The willingness to apologise is crucial.

Alan Southgate is a musician, music tutor and podcaster from the UK. He can be found online at Facebook.com/alan.southgate1.

Art Carden
Economics Professor, Alabama, USA

A word of introduction: I'm an economics professor at Samford University. I was awarded tenure effective August 2015. I've won awards for my research on Walmart, economic development, and economic history, and I've appeared in a lot of videos for the Institute for Humane Studies' LearnLiberty project.[3] At Samford, I teach Principles of Macroeconomics, Intermediate

---

[3] Found online at http://www.learnliberty.org/

Macroeconomics, and the MBA course "Economics of Competitive Strategy." Before joining the faculty at Samford, I taught at Rhodes College in Memphis, Tennessee where I taught the introductory economics course, economic history, Classical & Marxian Political Economy, and Public Choice. My life is soaked in academic pursuits and the liberal arts, and I'm an unschooling father of three.

While we lived in Memphis my wife and I decided we wanted to homeschool. As our son Jacob approached "school age," we did a lot of reading and, after watching a discussion between Stefan Molyneux and David Friedman, decided to take the unschooling plunge. As of this writing Jacob would be preparing to enter second grade. His sister Taylor Grace would be getting ready for Kindergarten, and his brother David (who just turned three) would be navigating that strange space between toddlerhood and school age that I've sometimes heard called "pre-K."

My wife and I come from decidedly non-radical educational backgrounds. We both graduated from public high schools, we met at the University of Alabama, and were married while I was a graduate student at Washington University in Saint Louis. We are both readers: I learned at an early age that when we went to visit my paternal grandparents the conversations between my father and grandfather were going to be about books and ideas (my grandfather was a Southern Baptist minister and later editor of the Bible Book Series for the Sunday School Board in Nashville). To make a long story short, I grew up in a house full of books and today own... a house full of books.

My evolving theory on an unschooling life emphasizes conversation, adaptation, and change. As an economist profoundly influenced by Adam Smith and Friedrich Hayek, I think state or national "standards" for what constitutes a sixth grade or an eighth grade or a twelfth grade education are unwise. I understand wanting to see that no child is left behind, but when I think about how much schooling and learning have changed since I finished graduate school, I don't think we can learn apart from experience, and experiment what the Right Standards are for students inhabiting innumerable cultural, political, moral, and intellectual contexts from sea to shining sea. When I graduated high school in 1997, none of the people working so hard to prepare me for the jobs of tomorrow told me I would need a social media strategy.

I'm also convinced that a lot of the time people spend in classrooms is being wasted. This is true at all levels, from Kindergarten through college. Graduate school, incidentally, is my model for an ideal educational experience. The seminar atmosphere was, to use a phrase I've heard before, "unrehearsed intellectual adventure." As an economics professor, I am learning that almost all of the information transfer parts of schooling can be outsourced to online video: why do I need to give a lecture on comparative advantage to my principles of macroeconomics students when I've already taught the lesson in a handful of LearnLiberty.org videos? Why do I need to give a lecture on the things that shift demand curves when students can watch a video from the authors of my textbook that features much better production values than I'm able to achieve with a whiteboard and markers?

It would be a huge mistake, I think, to infer from this that the professoriate is obsolete. I'm learning from my experience teaching online courses that my role is not as a gatekeeper of and conduit for the Wisdom of the Ages—students can get that from Wikipedia. My role is to help them take baby steps into the Great Conversation—to help them ask and answer their own questions about the ideas they have encountered. I'm there to help them contextualize and apply the ideas, and I'm also there to serve as something of an intellectual disc jockey—a term I get from Tyler Cowen's 2008 book *Create Your Own Economy*—working to curate content. Instead of holding forth about the things that shift demand curves, I'm there now to help students figure out what to read and watch and how to make sense of what they are reading and watching. The Internet has made demonstrations and explanations (audio and visual) available at very low cost for people who might need to encounter an idea two or three times or in two or three ways before they really get it. My role in the college classroom has changed.

As it is at Samford, so it is at home. There will always be in any circle those who are More Radical Than Thou, and we're still as of this writing attached to bedtimes and brushing teeth and encouraging the kids to eat what's on their plate, and we might have more expectations of our kids than the most radical of unschoolers (we're still learning; be patient with us). We've provided soft incentives for academic stuff like reading lessons, but by and large we let the kids explore wherever their imaginations take them. We do a lot of experiments and take a lot of trips, and I can't begin to explain how great it is to be able to get up in the morning and not be in a huge hurry to get the kids ready for school.

Our kids learn by navigating their world online and off—I was about to write "real world" and "virtual world," but I don't see how the kids' experiences in an electronic space are any less "real" than their experiences walking down a sidewalk apart from mere linguistic convention. Our oldest is a Minecraft expert. He refers to it as his "work"; indeed, one morning after he got out of bed I asked if I could have a hug and he responded "sorry, I have a lot of work to do" as he rubbed his still-sleepy eyes and walked to the computer.

It's clear he's learning a lot. First, he's able to solve pretty impressive design problems. He watches a lot of YouTube videos about this mod and that. Sometimes he uses a video to reproduce something he finds neat; sometimes he takes what he sees and modifies it, sometimes he comes up with something new. Second, he is being socialized (there's every homeschooler/unschooler's least favorite word) by learning how to deal with friends and family members who like Minecraft and some who would rather talk about something else. Third, our relationship is stronger (if not tested frequently) because a lot of the things he wants to do are a little beyond his ability and he therefore needs me to download and install some of the stuff he wants to use. His favorite question now is "will you look it up, please?"

I see the same pattern in his younger siblings. For my daughter, it's Disney Princesses and My Little Pony. For our youngest it's fire trucks, construction, Bob the Builder, and Teenage Mutant Ninja Turtles. I find it important—if not always easy—to be deliberate about taking an interest in the things they want to do. Playing Minecraft with Jacob over our home network can be a lot of fun. Going to see Disney on Ice was neat, and I've come to grips with the fact that I'm probably going to become a "Brony" because of the time I spend with my daughter. Not long ago, I took our youngest to a fire chief's convention because the convention organizers were kind enough to say "come on down" when I asked whether I could bring him to look around the exhibit hall. We are able to travel regularly without having to worry about taking the kids out of school. These aren't in addition to their educations. These experiences are their educations.

We're blessed because I make enough money to support our family comfortably on a single income; furthermore, academia offers me an incredible amount of flexibility that I wouldn't have with a 9-5 job. This allows me to take a very active role in the kids' lives, shuttling them back and forth between appointments, for example, taking them to dinner so my wife can have a break, or even taking one of them to the office with me.

That notwithstanding it is still very difficult to fight those fears that pop up from time to time about whether we are doing the right thing. Are our kids going to be messed up? What if we ruin them forever? What will the neighbors say? Then I remember how much I want to learn, how much I want to explore, and how much fun we're all having because I can take the kids along for the ride.

Unschooling isn't easy—far from it. You're talking about a lot of trips to the library, and a lot of time spent answering questions with what are too often unsatisfying answers ("son, we can't do that because it requires computer programming I don't know how to do"). The reward, though, is worth it. You get to see your children not as projects or as chunks of raw material that need to be fashioned into cogs for the social machine. You start to see them as apprentices and partners on an exploration of a wide and wild world and universe. It's a lot more fun than spelling worksheets, and I suspect the rewards will be a lot greater, too.

Art Carden is Associate Professor of Economics at Samford University in Birmingham, Alabama. His commentaries and research have appeared in Forbes, USA Today, *the* Washington Examiner, *and a range of regional and national publications. He lives in Birmingham with his wife Shannon and their three children Jacob, Taylor Grace, and David. He can be found online at Facebook.com/artcardeneconomist.*

Danilo Cuellar
Massage Therapist, New York, USA

Growing up my mother had always been the guiding force in my life, encouraging me to dig deeper and question things when necessary, always within the framework of the system, of course. As I proceeded through my 12 years of public schooling I first started thinking differently when, at the urging of a fellow budding revolutionary trapped in the system, I read

Hyperspace: A Scientific Odyssey Through Parallel Universes, Time Warps, and the 10th Dimension by Michio Kaku in 7th grade. This marked the beginning of my intellectual transformation at 12 years old when I started reading and learning extensively in the fields of chess, piano, theoretical physics, astronomy, cosmology, Eastern/Western philosophy, holistic nutrition, holistic medicine, and more. In 9th grade I started my own chess club, which was in effect until I graduated, after which it was disbanded due to lack of cohesive interest. My contrarian views irritated many of my teachers, although admittedly a select few of them did support my efforts to look beyond the accepted genres.

Today I write on the topics of political philosophy and economics. I also have a Facebook page and YouTube channel. I interview interesting people about political and educational philosophy, as well some solo video podcasts of just me speaking on the various topics mentioned above.

I have been working as an acupuncturist for nine years. I left my clinic in June of 2014 to be a full time unschooling father with my kids. I have a 5-year-old son and 3-year-old daughter. We are not planning on any more kids as of yet.

ON THEIR UNCONVENTIONAL APPROACH TO EDUCATION

Before having kids my wife and I both casually agreed, without giving it much thought, that we would spank our kids if they misbehaved. This was a conclusion arrived at more due to the appeal to antiquity and appeal to popularity than from careful research and investigation into the matter. Thankfully before my son reached his first birthday we discovered the science on the effects of spanking which gave us both an intellectual wake up call.[4] Since then I have been an unwavering outspoken advocate for peaceful parenting, attachment parenting, anti-spanking, and anti-circumcision. I firmly believe that one of the most effective ways to bring about a positive change in the world is to raise a generation of peaceful, compassionate, loving, rational, empathetic individuals! Let's outbreed the evil and wicked of the world! Let's drown them in love and kindness!

I first learned of unschooling through John Holt, Dayna Martin, John Taylor Gatto, and a few other of my influences. Then I started reading some books on homeschooling and unschooling. My wife and I are generally on board together with the concept. I absolutely adore the idea of passion-driven or child-driven education. I have come to

---

[4] See the Research page of Project NoSpank at http://skyler.link/nospankresearch

realize that children are not blank slates on which we must feverishly imprint our needs, wants, and desires lest they go through life stupid, barren, and destitute. Rather I now view them as unique and exceptional individuals with their own needs, wants, and desires entirely independent of my own. They will thrive not because of me, but in spite of me. I can choose to either encourage their natural development and proclivities or I can choose to be a barrier in the way of their burgeoning creativity and imagination. Genius is as common as dirt! The best thing we can do for our children is to get out of their way. A child who does not want to learn, nothing will convince him. A child who wants to learn, nothing will stop him!

Danilo Cuellar is a 32 years old acupuncturist, Chinese herbalist, Eastern nutritionist, and massage therapist. He can be found online at Facebook.com/danilo.cuellar.3.

David Martin
Business Owner, Florida, USA

With a 7-yr-old (and another on the way), how children (and adults) learn has been of great interest to me for a number of years now. I've tried to be as objective as possible and seek out the most evidence-based information on the topic. My wife and I have had to adjust our parenting approach many times after assessing studies and our daughter's tendencies, temperament and age. Many of the things I have come to realize have made me reflect on my own motivations (or lack thereof) to learn.

Something perhaps more controversial that I've concluded recently is that the learning conditions in which most children thrive is almost opposite of those found in compulsory education systems (most schools).

When our daughter began Kindergarten in the fall of 2013, we started having concerns when we noticed that so much of what we had learned about early childhood development and evidence regarding how children learn best was mostly being ignored in the school environment. Even worse, many policies and procedures appeared to go against what experts would advise based on solid data. Such as:

- Pushing academics too early;
- Too much focus on behavior management using a system that publicly shames and causes stigma, embarrassment, anxiety, gossip and confusion;
- Homework for young children;
- Extensive sitting, limited movement;
- Not enough outside time;
- Not enough free play;
- Too much focus on performance;
- Too much focus on competition, rather than cooperation;
- Rewards for conformity and obedience;
- Creativity, curiosity and individuality discouraged;
- Use of unnecessary extrinsic rewards;
- Food (candy) rewards;
- Unhealthy food choices;
- Yelling at children and other authoritarian tactics;
- Unfair and overused punishments;
- Excessive screen time;
- Focus on test preparation;
- Over-testing;
- Age segregation;

- Labeling individuals or groups as "bad," "good," or other unnecessary labeling;
- Reduction of family time, secure attachment;
- Outdated materials;
- Stressful situations.

For younger children, my biggest takeaway from looking at the evidence was that:

- Children learn best through free self-directed play;
- The ability for children to learn can be severely hindered by stress and anxiety;
- When she attended public school kindergarten the environment was stressful and there was a lack of time for free play. Not good!

Despite these conditions, our daughter did fine at first. She adapted. She had her best friend in class. She stayed on "green." She did her homework. But as time went on, we could tell that the creative spark, the sense of wonder, and the desire to learn was starting to wane. Our list of concerns grew. The novelty of school was dissipating for her while the anxiety and stress caused by the system was becoming apparent. Finally, enough was enough and we pulled her out in January of 2014.

We began doing something we once thought we'd never consider, home-based education! Although we had our doubts along the way, we were soon seeing signs that this could be a great fit for all of us. We focused on the fact that she was her own person that can learn at her own pace and we had to trust her and the process.

After a few months of homeschooling, I asked our daughter about her memories of public school, and she replied: "They just taught us what NOT to do. Now I'm learning all the things I CAN do." Wow. How telling is that. This was justification that this particular school was not an ideal learning environment for her.

We now have over one year of near-unschooling under our belt and completed our first annual evaluation in January of 2015. While preparing her portfolio we were blown away when we saw just how much learning she experienced in one year. But more importantly, it wasn't as much about what we did as what we now saw in our daughter. The excitement to learn was back and greater than ever. Her interests are varied and vast. From disassembling computers to raising praying mantises; chess to art; anatomy to magic; volleyball to video editing; managing her money to running a dog walking business; exploring in the woods to quiet time with books. She would never have had time to pursue all these various interests if she was attending a regular school, completing the required homework, and helping with chores. School didn't do anything but get in her way of real learning. School creates a ceiling. A subject she may master in an hour or two might be repeated for weeks. She might be ready to move on to bigger and better things, but would instead be bored and disengaged. On the flip-side, if she wanted to spend more time on a topic that was of incredible interest to her or needed more time to master, that was impossible or difficult within the school environment.

Now not all schools are equal. There are some great alternative schools and other organized learning options available. Our daughter attends weekly enrichment programs, co-ops, homeschooling programs, field trips and events. There are also dual-enrollment opportunities available if needed.

Some may wonder about socialization. That was a total non-issue. We found that there are so many opportunities for unschooled kids to socialize with kids of all ages (and adults) that it allows for a broader and more realistic social atmosphere. Her socialization in school was restricted to a short recess and rushed lunchtime.

We have no idea if we will always unschool, but for now our daughter is quite content. She enjoys learning and understands that we are there to support her path to greater knowledge, achievement and happiness.

David Martin is the founder, owner and operator of the technology company Brighter Technologies, Inc. He is a self-taught developer with a primary focus on website and database development. He is an avocational scientist who enjoys spending time outdoors studying biodiversity with children. He is married with 2 children and resides in Southwest Florida. He can be found online at facebook.com/dimossi.

Edwin Stanton
Sports News Editor, Alabama, USA

As my job title suggests, I have a passion for sports. I've been around sports my whole life and working at the newspaper has brought me a lot of joy through the years.

I have one child who is 10 years old. Elliot is not interested in sports at all. While I'm a little disappointed he doesn't share my love of sports, it has not taken away from our father-son relationship. He shows an interest in a wide variety of subjects, such as animals – wolves in particular. At age 7 he informed his mother and me he intends to be a wolf biologist.

I think the fact he knows what career path he wants to follow is because of his home-based education. Had he been going to public school on a daily basis, I don't believe he would have been able to discover what his passions were. He was able, on his own, to discover his passion for wolves and study the subject in depth. Homeschooling has been a wonderful advantage for Elliot. I didn't use to think that way. At all.

When Elliot was born, I naturally expected him to attend a public school, get involved in activities such as band, sports, and clubs, or maybe in student government. That's how I was raised and everyone else I know was raised. In fact, I had never met a homeschooling parent or child before.

The homeschooling idea was brought to me by my wife, Tiffany, who had been researching it on the Internet. She had a son, Trey, who was in public school, and she had concerns about putting Elliot through the same ordeal. Every day, it seemed, she would tell me all the trouble Trey was having in school. The trouble wasn't that Trey had difficulties learning, rather, it was the fact the school was not doing enough to educate him. By the time he was in fourth grade, Trey had lost interest in school and learning altogether. It wasn't fun and it seemed like this horrible chore that had to be endured for eight hours a day, just like a job.

My wife didn't want that for Elliot and she did her best to convince me that homeschooling was the way to give Elliot the best education possible. I was adamantly against it. I was a product of the public education system and was able to attend college and get a job. Why couldn't Elliot do the same? I couldn't understand why it was so difficult to realize that public school had plenty of benefits.

Learning the Ropes

The biggest concern I had was the actual learning part. I'm not a teacher and neither is my wife. How in the world was I going to teach my son about math, science, literature or history? I'm not qualified to do those things.

ON THEIR UNCONVENTIONAL APPROACH TO EDUCATION

After much discussion of the idea, I relented and we began the journey of home-based education. At first it was easy. When kids are young, you are just teaching the basics — numbers, letters, shapes, colors, etc. This is the age they soak up all the information, and this type of education was required of me as a parent to teach him anyway.

When we began doing more advanced stuff, like reading, simple math, and an introduction to science, I began to get worried. My struggle was not with Elliot learning the topics, but with me giving the instruction and teaching the material. There are several ways to educate at home, and the method we chose was a combination of unschooling and other relaxed methods. I began introducing material to Elliot and we discussed it at length over the course of several days until he was able to grasp it fully. We did this with all subjects and material and I found that we didn't just discuss it during times of learning, but we talked about it in the car, at the grocery store, while watching TV or when were just hanging out together.

I began to realize that school was in session all day, even if we weren't in a classroom or sitting at a desk. I think that's what sold me on the whole thing. When a kid is in school he is there to learn and once the bell rings, learning time is over. With unschooling, the opportunity to learn is ongoing and is not restricted to a schedule.

Because of this, we were able to spend our time focused on a particular piece of material and stick with it for as long as we wanted. In public school, there isn't enough time to devote to one thing because they have to follow a guideline. When Elliot was having difficulty with math, we were able to put everything else away and just stick with math until he felt comfortable with it.

Social Life

Another concern for me was friends. How in the world would Elliot interact with other kids if he was at home and not around other boys and girls his own age? My fears were put to rest early in Elliot's unschooling development. We got involved in many activities and groups to support our unschooling endeavors and got to know many parents and kids along the way. It didn't take long to realize that other homeschooled kids attended the same groups, camps and events as we did. Elliot made many friends along the way, including his best friend Max.

He is not receiving the same form of social interaction as 'regular' kids in public school, and I do realize Elliot is different from those kids, as he hasn't been exposed to them and the culture that comes with public school. Elliot does get to meet a much more eclectic group of people, however. They have allowed Elliot to be himself, without the repercussions of being teased or mocked. Everyone in the group was a little different and everyone was OK with that. Elliot has even stated to me that he knows he is not like other kids and is a little weird. But he is OK with that. This fact, above anything else we have benefited from unschooling, is the most satisfying. I felt pressure to fit in and be with the in-crowd in school. I didn't dare share my true feelings for something until the rest of the group was OK with it. If it was considered 'stupid' or 'lame' to do something, I didn't do it. Elliot doesn't care. He knows who he is and is fine with it. He has long hair and dresses pretty weird and goes out in public wearing a soldier's helmet. He gets stares from people in restaurants, and gets called 'a girl' all the time due to his long hair, but he's perfectly fine with it and takes it all in stride. I know that's a direct correlation to him being unschooled.

The Future

Although I see positive results with unschooling, I still am not 100 percent certain of

Elliot's future. I still have concerns, mainly with college and how Elliot will be accepted and whether or not we are teaching him all he needs to know.

We are working on a plan to help us with those concerns, but there are still a lot of issues we have and some doubts as to whether we are doing right by Elliot and his future. He's behind in his reading skills, and his writing skills leave much to be desired. We are hoping these issues will be small bumps in the road and not cause trouble when he's older.

I know he's a smart kid because he educates me on some things that I don't know and when he learns something, he learns it. It's not just retained for a week and forgotten. Overall, I'm totally for unschooling. Like I say, I still have some doubts, but the results are conclusive that it was right for us. Elliot is a happy child who has flourished from this method of education.

Edwin Stanton is the Sports Managing Editor for The Tuscaloosa News in Alabama. He can be found online at Facebook.com/edwin.stanton.777.

ON THEIR UNCONVENTIONAL APPROACH TO EDUCATION

Jeff Till
Entrepreneur, South Carolina, USA

Dear dads, please don't make the same heinous mistake I made. I sent my kids to public school without even thinking about it for five minutes. Upon our children reaching kindergarten age, my wife made the arrangements to enroll my children in the public school nearest our house. We took them to the bus stop, the bus showed up, the kids got on, off went the bus, and that was it.

We unschool now, which is really a way of saying we don't send them to school anymore. Unschooling isn't really a form of schooling; in my vernacular it's a word that means *freedom for children*. We let our kids be free and they choose, like free people, what to do with their time and resources. Those are the activities that make them happy, interested, and engaged.

The decision to stop schooling came after an intensive period of research and analysis. I read a half dozen books on education, listened to a lot of education and philosophy podcasts, and did a ton of my own thinking about my children, my wife, myself and our current school. It probably took me close to a year to get a complete view of what I wanted for my children. I'll explain my whole experience a little later.

I believe you owe it to yourself and your children to do some really serious research, thinking and exploration before you decide to send your child to school (public or private) or recreate a school-like curriculum at home. The commitment to schooling is a 15,000 hour endeavor, spread over 13 years. And if it is a public school, it is administered by the government, where key decisions about your child are largely determined by a group of strangers to you who also don't know about the specific needs of your child. 15,000 hours is the equivalent time you would work at your job for seven and a half years. It's a huge decision, and even if the final analysis points to schooling your children, you'll feel better about making it if you did your due diligence. Plus, you'll be able to explain to your children in detail why you chose to put them in school or not. And you'll be equipped to explain to your wife your decision wherever you land.

So first, go out and explore a bunch of books and media.[5] If you are already on the side of schooling, you might skip materials that advocate

---

[5] Start with the "Further Reading" section at the end of this book.

for it. Or read books that are both critical and supportive of schooling if you feel it will give you a complete view. Also, learn what unschooling is, learn how it represents freedom and get comfortable with the concepts. Just do the research. It's fascinating stuff anyway.

Next, do some analysis and reflection. You are going to think about what is best for your children, or you may think about what's best for any child, but I'm going to suggest something different as a first step: think about yourself.

If you can't imagine yourself being free as a child, it's likely going to be impossible to think that your own children can be free. If the idea of yourself being free as a child is irresistible, then you can't deny it to your children.

I'm assuming you were sent to school, probably a public school, and have safely managed to become a functioning adult capable of supporting a household and understanding how to raise and interact with children.

First, reflect on how you acquired knowledge that you either found useful (e.g., like the skills you use for work) or enjoyable (e.g., the stuff you like to learn, for me its economics, playing music and NFL football.) How much of this did you learn in school? Beyond basic reading and some simple math, I bet it will not be much. And, almost none of the essential skills of living (e.g., driving a car, cooking a meal, applying for a loan) are taught in school. That's because they are too important to learn.

What you did learn were complicated math problems, detailed science fields you may or may not have liked, sentence diagraming, memorizing the spelling of words, political histories, state capitals, 18th century literature and an entire portfolio of stuff you likely found mostly useless or unenjoyable.

And you forgot most of it anyway.

Now imagine picking your own topics and having all of that glorious time to explore those that either provided real value or real enjoyment. By age 12 you may have been an expert in several exotic topics. You may have built something valuable. Maybe even generated income and gained real world experience. Imagine the opportunity to have those 15,000 hours back to accomplish what you desired to do. Think of the head start you would've had in life. Imagine getting 15,000 hours back when you were the most curious, the most energetic, the most optimistic, and the most risk-resilient person you ever were.

If you would have flourished with that time back, even just slightly more than you did at school, then imagine it for your kids.

Now think about your own happiness when you were schooled. Did you like it? Or was most of it kind of boring and stressful? Did you like your evenings being filled up with homework? Did you like getting a report card? Did you like taking tests? Did you enjoy filling out endless worksheets? Did you like riding the bus? Did you care for how your teachers and many of the children treated you?

How often did you yearn for summer vacation? School isn't enjoyable or happy. It sucks. Given the choice, would you retroactively inflict this massive quantity of unhappiness on yourself? Think about this one long and hard, because it was when I developed this sense of empathy for my children's happiness did I reach the tipping point.

You can do this self-analysis on a wide variety of points. Some of them include thinking about[6]:

- How school creates conformity, obedience and apathy;
- How school limits subjects and ignores some really good ones;

---

[6] Read "A Complete Case for Home Education (54 Arguments)" by the author at http://skyler.link/homeeducation54

- How testing and grades stink;
- How school separates families for most of the waking day;
- How it screws up vacations and free time;
- How it doesn't prepare for a career very well;
- How it made you tired and robbed you of rest/sleep.

In hearing about unschooling, you may be barraged with all of the practical, beneficial reasons why unschooling makes sense, such as it fosters better learning or it lets children discover themselves in better ways (it's true.) Or you may hear about how the public school system was designed by nineteenth century Prussians to make obedient soldiers (also true).

But I think a father can only be convinced of unschooling's merits if the father can imagine himself succeeding if he had been free as a child. It's a tough analysis to be sure. The biggest blockade is that you were probably broken by your own schooling. It robbed you of the sense that a child can be free and still flourish. It taught you that hardship and meaningless, droning tasks are our state of nature. In order to unschool your children, you need, to some extent, to deschool yourself. You need to reverse the indoctrination you suffered. You need to first free yourself of the concept and then you can free your children.

My Path to Unschooling My Children

I've long heard the intellectual arguments against schooling and the arguments for homeschooling. I knew, intellectually, that compulsory school was a bad thing, but it wasn't something I thought about much, even after my children were born.

When my oldest daughter was school-aged, my wife and I put her on the bus to the nearest public school like all of our neighbors did, like my parents did with me, and like my wife's parents had done to her. When my son reached that age, we did the same thing.

I hated putting them on that bus. It made me feel kind of lousy every morning. Then the house would be kind of dead and lifeless for most of the day with them gone (I work at home and my wife is a full-time mom.) Things felt better again when they came home. But then there was homework, which they didn't like. My wife would get frustrated and tell me to help them, but I didn't want to. It was boring for both my children and me and it ate into our precious Nintendo Wii time together. Plus, I had never bothered doing homework myself as a child and never really saw the point. The evenings were too short to do much. Between homework, a meal, and having to go to bed super early to make tomorrow's bus, there was very little family time.

As time went on, I started to examine aspects of my life that I found unpleasant and thought about ways to get rid of them. Some of the things I would do included shortening my workweek drastically and putting our New England house on the market to move to a warmer climate (freedom from snow!).

I caught John Taylor Gatto's "The Ultimate History Lesson" on the Internet and found it fascinating.[7] In the five hour video, he explains the origination and true purpose of school. I really started to think about how schooling was another unhappy, deleterious thing that I could get rid of.

Still, I wasn't ready to do it and every part of me resisted the idea. I thought nobody homeschooled except crazies who quilt and think Adam walked around with dinosaurs six thousand years ago. Plus, I had gone to public school. Everybody has to. It's a state of nature. It's automatic. It's undeniable.

---

[7] See "The Ultimate History Lesson: A Weekend with John Taylor Gatto" at http://skyler.link/thultimate

But, I was still fascinated by the subject so I started feasting on books, starting with two by John Taylor Gatto, then Grace Llewellyn[8] and later John Holt.[9] I also visited homeschooling blogs and online discussion boards. I was also listening to the Freedomain Radio podcast daily, which was often critical of schooling.

My wife saw my night table reading stack and was getting either nervous or curious. I asked her to read Gatto's *Dumbing Us Down*, and she did.[10] She agreed with everything in the book, but like me, wasn't ready to take the kids out of school.

As my analysis grew, I started looking into homeschooling curriculum and tools. There's a tremendous market for homeschooling text books and even wholly packaged school-at-home programs available. One piece we got was a detailed catalog of the Calvert curriculum, which comes with everything you need to replicate school at home short of the apple for the teacher's desk. I was getting familiar with unschooling concepts, but the idea that we could simply buy a homeschool

---

[8] Read *The Teenage Liberation Handbook* by Grace Llewellyn; available in paperback at http://skyler.link/amznteenlib
[9] You can find John Holt's library of books at http://skyler.link/holtbooks
[10] Available in several formats at http://skyler.link/amzndumbing

program was comforting in some ways. It made my wife and I feel less helpless and alone, even if replicating school at home wasn't the right thing to do.

I also researched the state's homeschooling laws. I figured they would be intimidating and I was confounded at the start, presuming I'd find it frustrating. But it wasn't, and the more I learned about the legal aspects, the more comfortable I became.

All of this reading and researching was absolutely necessary to understand what was available. The more I learned, the more I was able to create a rigorous intellectual case for home schooling.

The full intellectual case wasn't enough though. I still couldn't imagine doing it.

Over the course of late 2012 and most of 2013 my mother was being ravaged by cancer. I talked to her on the phone every day to hear her complain and stressfully explain her fear and frustration. She just got worse and worse. I visited her at the hospital for the last few days she could still speak and was conscious. She died on October 28th, 2013.

On the same day of her death, we got our first offer on our house. The house had been on the market for over two years without an offer, postponing our move to South Carolina.

I had to negotiate the selling of the house over the two days of my mother's wake and funeral. It was an awful offer and between that and the death I was an emotional and stressful wreck. Plus the trip included visiting my sickly father and seeing a hundred weeping relatives and family friends I hadn't seen in decades. Plus I was going to be moving in six weeks, had a house to pack, a new house to find across the country and everything else that goes with moving far away. I was a hot mess emotionally.

On the morning of my mother's funeral, I was driving to the funeral parlor and was just absolutely weeping as hard as I ever had in my life. Life was vicious and short at that moment. In this emotional state my senses of risk, decision-making and view of reality was completely unguarded.

I suddenly realized that we had to homeschool because there was no way I would send myself to school understanding what I knew about school. If faced with the choice, I wouldn't make myself unhappy, I wouldn't waste my time, I wouldn't put myself through the torture of school. With any empathy, how dare I send my children? How dare I treat them in a way that I wouldn't treat myself?

I called my wife and let her know that I really wanted to do it. She agreed tentatively. A couple weeks later she would visit our new South Carolina town to scout a house. She visited the elementary school and there were dozens of trailers behind the school in rows surrounded by high wire fences. These were make-shift classrooms because of the school being overcrowded. It looked like a prison. This helped cement her decision to homeschool.

By mid-December, we sold our home, sent the moving van off and started driving to South Carolina. Shortly after we moved in we met several other home schooling families and became friends. They largely unschooled. While we had bought a load of academic books and courses, we decided to not actively use them. School-like books would be available to my children, but not actively forced upon them. We tried an online education program, but the kids found it boring. After a few weeks of not going to school and not having school at home, we began to get comfortable in the unschool life. It was working and everyone was happier.

A Day in the Unschool Life,
or **A Day In the Life of a Free Family**

We've been at it for about 18 months now. My children are ages 10, 7 and 4 at the writing of this story. The results aren't in on how effective unschooling is as an educative process (which isn't really the point), and who knows what we'll do in the future, but we really like it. The kids can't even imagine going back to school, even though they never once questioned why they originally had to go in the first place.

We don't do much at all. Everyone gets up in the morning sometime after 8:30 (compare to the school kids here who have to get up at 5:30 to make the bus.) We have breakfast together as a family. I then go check work email and the kids go to their computers or toys to play. I like to go to the swimming pool to do laps in the morning and the family usually meets me there. We have lunch together. The afternoons vary with meeting up with other home school friends, going to horseback riding, flag football, dance class and Tae Kwon Do lessons. Or sometimes they just play inside or outside. Or we'll go to the beach. Or the movies. Or my daughter will read a book. Maybe they'll paint for a bit. My oldest daughter likes to bake and do some of her own grocery shopping. Whatever they feel like doing. Sometimes they watch television, but not as much as you'd think.

I work in my home office during the weekday afternoons. They often come in if they need help and I'll come down frequently to see how everybody is doing. Sometimes I show them what I'm working on. Sometimes I skip work for a beach trip or to nap with the four-year-old.

In the evening they try to play with school friends back from the grind. This is hit or miss because the school kids have to do homework and be in bed early to catch the next day's bus. Many of them go to latchkey type programs, so their nights are very short.

After dinner I usually play football or basketball with my son. Than around 8:30 the whole family lounges into our king size bed and we watch a movie together. It's not uncommon for the kids to stay up until 10:30 or so. It doesn't matter though, because we do whatever we want.

They have a few chores. My oldest daughter does her own laundry, helps with shopping and sometimes prepares lunch for her siblings. She bakes and cooks. My son cleans up dog poop. They have to pick up their rooms now and again. There's not really anything in terms of discipline. We don't do timeouts or withhold things they like, and we certainly don't spank. If they do something that displeases us, we let them know and work towards a resolution.

The legal stuff for homeschooling is easy. It takes about 10 minutes per year of clicking on two electronic forms to get that done.

One thing that hasn't happened are the wonder stories that unschoolers sometimes tell, such as a child launching his own business or building a working particle collider. My kids are still young, so they mostly play.

I also wish more, if not all, families would unschool. We're able to hook up with other families, do some classes, and find school kids to play with on the weekends, but it would be better if there were more kids around. At this time, 97% of children are locked up in school for the majority of the week. Even if the number of homeschoolers jumped from three percent to say ten percent, we'd have a lot more opportunities for playtime. This isn't to say that school does a better job at providing playmates, because it doesn't (kids at school are told to sit and be quiet most of the day,) it's just that the population of homeschool kids is pretty anemic right now.

The Final Personal Argument from Experimentation and Low Risk

The final case for unschooling is the easiest to justify: try it. There's almost no risk. Take a few months or maybe a year and try it out. Don't like it? You can always go back to public school. The administrators will welcome your child back with open arms and gladly tell your children to get back in line and shut their mouths. The public school won't disappear this year or next.

Experiment and see what happens. See if you and your children are happier. See if you enjoy more family time and the conveniences unschooling provides. See if engagement and curiosity reemerge.

After all, you would probably let yourself try it had you been given the chance.

Thanks for reading, and peace!

Jeff is a professional writer and business owner of a firm specializing in thought leadership development for the management consulting and enterprise technology industry. His hobbies include studying ethics, economics, education, history and other topics. He can be found online at Facebook.com/jtfhy.

John Durso
Business Owner, California, USA

The first time I heard the term "Unschooling" was in a talk given by Debbie Harbeson at the 2011 Libertopia conference in San Diego, CA where she gave me a copy of her book: *Okay Kids, Time For Bedlam*. My wife Kelly and I devoured her book, hit Youtube looking for more, and found "Astra Taylor on the Unschooled Life," a lecture given at the Walker Art Center in 2009[11]; Kelly credits the video with "sealing the deal" for her.

Before our first son was born, Kelly was a biology teacher at a public high school; in her few years working within 'the system' she worked to establish a culture of mutual respect and individual personhood which the students seemed to really be starving for. Once our oldest son was born, Kelly decided to be a stay-at-home mom. I run a fire protection company with ~75 employees which unfortunately doesn't afford me as much time at home as I'd like, but I try to make every moment count. After the kids are asleep we sometimes find ourselves staying up late discussing the finer

---

[11] View on YouTube at http://skyler.link/astrataylorul

implications of the non-aggression principle[12] in our parenting lives. It's easy to become discouraged as an aspiring 'peaceful parent' when you fall short of your expectations when tensions rise; it's exceptionally difficult to manage the needs, safety, and desires of five individuals (too often parents forget to count themselves among those who require care), but if you picture 'peaceful parenting' not as an end to be achieved, but rather a goal to be aspired towards, it's easier to take pride in the small successes of everyday life.

Kelly and I look back at our years in public school and marvel at how little we've retained even from some of our favorite classes. Kelly's experience differed from mine insofar as she was driven to get straight A's, keen on pleasing others, whereas I applied myself to the subjects which interested me, and only did enough to get by in those which did not. My knack for test taking helped me earn good enough grades to be admitted to the University of Colorado at Boulder, where, in retrospect, I pursued my own version of unschooling without knowing what to call it. I got to know my professors and engaged them outside

---

[12] See the Wikipedia entry for "Non-aggression Principle" at http://skyler.link/wikinap

of the classroom, intent on taking from them the knowledge I wanted with little regard for their lesson plans.

I'm very excited to see my kids learning what they want to learn when they want to learn it. Once you've opened your mind to the idea that kids want to learn the things they need to know in order to do what they want to do, compulsory education looks insane. My oldest son got really interested in numbers when he was about two to when he was four; he was counting, then adding, finally multiplying, but then just lost interest and moved on to something else. It just seemed like such a natural way to learn; by stark contrast the schooling model of learning six different subjects simultaneously in prescribed blocks of time marked by bells really seems detrimental to any real learning and long term retention.

We feel given the realizations we've made we couldn't live with ourselves forcing our kids to go to school, although there is the persistent fear of being all alone. We had a handful of families all with boys of similar ages to ours we saw on a regular basis, then as their kids started going to preschool, we drifted apart. Unfortunately as time wears on, our oldest son grows more bored and lonely in 'baby groups'. We have two families we're still close to, but they're not completely committed to an alternative to school. So at this point we are seeking out other unschooling families with which to build our community.

John Durso is a business owner, running a fire protection company with several dozen employees. He can be found online at Facebook.com/john.j.durso.5.

Pace Ellsworth
Entrepreneur, Arizona, USA

My name is Pace. I have a wife and two kids; my boy is five, my girl is three. I run a small marketing consulting company in the financial industry. I'm lucky enough to work from home as an entrepreneur and pursue my dreams. The life I love is this: playing together with my family, learning languages, talking about religion and technology, meeting new people, and playing video games. We are unschoolers.

My family is the center of my world. I have awesome parents, and so does my wife. As kids, they let us do what we wanted to do. No curfews, no time outs, no punishments. They did that because they taught us safety and how to make our own decisions and they respected our decisions and helped us if we made mistakes. Growing up, they loved us for who we were, not who they wanted us to be. This made it a lot easier to accept radical, whole life unschooling when we finally got it.

We definitely wanted to parent the same way we were parented, but we had no idea when we got married or even after having our second kid that they would never go to school full-time. My wife and I both went through public and private schools, Kindergarten through 12th grade, but we never really fit there. We felt held back and boxed in. The classes were either too boring or too hard, and many of them felt like a waste of our time. Even so, that was the way people did childhood, so we didn't really question it at first.

As young parents, we were anxious to learn about what our options would be. We knew we didn't like our public education experiences, and didn't want that for our children. Soon we found TED talks and other media by people like Sugata Mitra and Sir Ken Robinson, who explained that set schedules and lessons stifle creativity in children, who will naturally self-organize and seek knowledge with just the most basic tools at their disposal.[13]

Then our kids started growing up and choosing things to learn. At the same time, we found groups online that introduced us to unschooling, and we realized that we were already unschooling! Just doing what we were doing, guiding our kids to learn motor skills, language skills, technology skills, was all we had to do... because they chose what to learn. I really want that dynamic for my whole life. I want them to have the freedom to pursue their passions instead of having their activities chosen for them forty or more hours a week. Their amazing and unique minds need to be respected with the freedom of choice.

I believe in zero restrictions on digital technology use for my family. We've seen the benefits far outweigh any possible negative effects it could have. So far our tech use has been a beautiful unifying factor for us, as it provides an instant connection to family members across the country and across the world, and of course a broad source of educational programming. And we are right by their side, watching, supporting, and

---

[13] View Ken Robinson's talks on TED.com at http://skyler.link/tedkrobinson; view Sugata Mitra's talks on TED.com at http://skyler.link/tedsmitra

learning with them. I hope that today's generation of parents doesn't lose touch with their children and grandchildren in the changing world that awaits us. Our children will know what to do since they are already creating that world that we'll be living in. Let's follow them.

Life, especially in the 21st century, is like an all-you can-eat buffet. You walk in every day and try a bunch of things. Most get into a routine of favorite foods and keep it at that, switching it up once in a while. Schooling, however, can be like having to go to a catered 3-course meal with tiny servings of the most boring foods that someone else chose that you don't like anyway. Maybe you get lucky and you like a few things. Maybe you're the type that likes everything they serve, but all the while you are kept away from the buffet of options you could have had. At the root of this is treating kids like we treat adults, and allowing them the freedom to choose what to learn.

Pace Ellsworth was born in Abu Dhabi, United Arab Emirates. After a church mission to Lima, Peru, he married his high school sweetheart and graduated from BYU in Linguistics, minors in Spanish and Linguistic Computing. Pace's interests include classical liberalism and futurism. He now lives in

Mesa, Arizona, with his wife and two children, where he works as a marketing consultant for small businesses in the technology and finance sectors. He can be found online at Facebook.com/paceme.

Rob Nielsen
Online Education and Training, Utah, USA

Being a good husband and father is the core of my life. I am a working professional, but I aspire to become financially independent. My wife and I have two children.

My experience with school and educational environments includes: "public" [government] k-12 schools (student, employee), homeschool (student and parent), charter schools (employee), non-accredited private k-12 schools (student), credit by examination (student), computer networking training company (student), missionary language training (student), private university (student), public university (student), online language course vendor (employee), for-profit online vocational training (employee), for-profit nursing college (employee), and not-for-profit online competency-based accredited university (employee).

I consider the proper education of my children to be my top priority. My children are currently 9 (girl) and 6 (boy). We provide an environment and opportunities to learn at home and in our community every day. We also travel, play, and explore things together. What we don't do is schedule time each day to do worksheets, memorize arbitrary lists of things, or demand compliance from our children. We treat them as individuals who deserve our respect, but happen to also require significant guidance from us in addition to the love and general support we offer. Since I am an experienced expert in education, curriculum, and assessment, I know what is best for my children, and that is freedom and assistance when asked.

Since I am at work during typical work hours, my wife is primarily responsible for supervising the children during the day. They are still young, but as they get older, they are becoming more and more responsible for their own goals and how they spend their time. I will become increasingly involved as they get into the teenage years, when we will have more serious discussions about what they want to do with their adult lives and how they can best prepare for the future.

One of our biggest challenges has been striking a balance between letting the kids be kids, providing opportunities to learn and grow, and over-scheduling or providing a structure that is too rigid. Part of the point of not going to a school is to learn to think for yourself, which includes self-awareness, responsibility, trial-and-error (also known as the scientific method), goal setting, and more. These things only truly develop to their potential in an environment of freedom and natural consequences. I think you could fairly consider us an unschooling family. We are also committed to peaceful parenting, which means that we consider ourselves coaches, mentors, and exemplars in our children's lives and do not resort to violent or manipulative consequences like physical punishment or shaming.

We have not encountered too much resistance in our choice to teach our children at home, and any concerns from friends and family are easily cleared up with just a few minutes of conversation.

I don't foresee any roadblocks, but I will honor the choices of my children as they grow. If they choose to be involved in some formal school activity, they are free to choose that. However, I doubt that the freedom and empowerment they experience at home will make them likely to choose to jump on a conveyor belt for long. It could also be a great learning experience in that it will provide contrast for what they have experienced at home and give more context and meaning to ongoing conversations about how the world works.

As part of showing that learning is just a natural part of a healthy life, I continue to pursue goals of my own, such as learning languages, organizing and building things, reading and writing regularly, playing music, and much more. My ultimate goal is that my children will be able to live independently and pursue truth and happiness in a lifestyle of their choosing. I will always be a part of empowering that whether my children live under my roof or not.

Rob Nielsen got his M.Ed in Instructional Technology and has been working in online education and training for about 10 years. He can be found online at Facebook.com/rob.nielsen.71.

Skyler Collins
Entrepreneur, Utah, USA

The thought of sending my children to school sends shivers down my spine. The reasons for this are many-fold, but primarily it is my commitment to raising my children without coercion or manipulation. My discovery of unschooling came just after my wife and I decided to raise our children without either punishments or rewards, but instead with connection, love, and reason.[14] My oldest, a son, was five at the time and experiencing his first year of school, pre-kindergarten. Since the time he was about three we would either put him in time-out or spank him in the attempt to "correct" his behavior that we didn't like. After a friend introduced us to Alfie Kohn's work on parenting, titled *Unconditional Parenting*[15], we decided that using punishments and rewards to discipline our children was not in their or our best interest.

Now that we've put away these punitive and manipulative tools, I was conflicted about the environment he was going to spend half his day in.

---

[14] Read "Post-Punitive Parenting" by the author at http://skyler.link/sjcpostpunitive
[15] Available in several formats at http://skyler.link/amznakup

That environment, the school environment, was built and is maintained with these discarded tools. I feared our work at home at disciplining our children with connection, love, and reason would be undone if he went to school. The two environments are antithetical to each other and the one antithetical to the culture of peace that we wanted to build. So I decided to search for alternatives.

My search first brought me to the more recent online-based options. Programs like K12 offer the schooling model over the Internet. I was intrigued. My children could do schooling but avoid most of the environment. Of course K12 still does grades (rewards), but it seemed like a step in the right direction. I was thinking very seriously about this alternative when a friend recommended I read a book about the homeschooling model that his family follows, titled *A Thomas Jefferson Education*, by Oliver DeMille.[16] I did so immediately. My excitement over what this book had to offer grew after every page. The "TJEd" philosophy is all about structuring time instead of content. It offered a vision of guiding your children toward their interests in various subjects as scheduled throughout the day, but not in choosing for them

---

[16] Available in several formats at http://skyler.link/amzntjed

what they will study within each subject. The parent's job was to schedule their child's day around the content they chose based on their own interests. It also stressed the inclusion of "classic" works throughout the year, I suppose through parental recommendation.

As I researched TJEd online, I came across the awkward yet edgy term of "unschooling." It immediately piqued my interest. I searched the term and discovered all sorts of amazing resources, the biggest of which was probably Sandra Dodd's website.[17] She had links to every unschooling and parenting topic under the sun, with a consistent theme running throughout: the absence of coercion and manipulation in the educational pursuits of children and adolescents. I felt like I'd found the holy grail of educational philosophy, but I had so many questions and concerns about things like reading levels, mathematics, the possibility of college, future jobs, state requirements, etc. I even had concerns about things like children and eating, sleeping, chores, and all the non-educational aspects of raising a family and maintaining a home. I found very interesting perspectives on all of these things at Sandra Dodd's site and others. How they talked about these concepts was completely new

---

[17] Visit SandraDodd.com

to me. It was obvious that they held a very different paradigm regarding these things than anything I'd ever experienced or heard about in my life.

I became less and less convinced that my children needed to be coerced or manipulated into learning or doing anything as they grew up. My job now was to pass on this new knowledge to my wife so that we could make the decision to give our children real choice together. I appreciated her skepticism toward this radical new (to us) idea of "unschooling" our children. Though she was reluctant to make such a drastic change, she nevertheless decided to trust that I was only trying to do what I thought was best for our children's futures. And we took the plunge at the beginning of my son's kindergarten. He attended for a week before we went on family vacation, at which time we explained to him his options and let him decide if he wanted to stay in school or come home and try unschooling. Needless to say he became a kindergarten dropout and has never even thought about going back. He's almost ten now and is living a very joyful, yet often challenging, life.

Last year my daughter was faced with the same choice toward going to pre-kindergarten or staying home and continuing the unschooling that she had lived with since birth. She decided to try it, probably after seeing how often school is heralded in many of her favorite television shows. (They never depict the boring hours-long classes or grueling homework, of course.) So we signed her up. A week before starting, she and my wife attended the orientation. The teacher explained the rules, such as raising your hand to speak. That must have struck the wrong chord with my daughter. You see as unschoolers we don't really live by rules, but rather principles, and so when she heard that she had to raise her hand if she wanted to do something as freely as speak, she didn't like that. The orientation filled her curiosity and she no longer had any interest in attending pre-kindergarten. It certainly helped that it was at this time that she began playing Minecraft with her big brother. She was entering the very exciting and very relevant world of computing. Both she and her brother are avid gamers and Googlers today.

These days our week is filled with computers, YouTube videos, television shows, video games, park days, play dates, library visits, museums, swimming, hiking, family vacations, and everything else that we feel like doing or exploring. My children have real control over their lives and the things they do and the knowledge they obtain.

They are very happy. Of course things break or don't work quite right and emotions sometimes run high, but we've all evolved to a real place of peace and life-long learning. Every day brings new challenges and new knowledge. My wife's reluctance has faded quite a bit now that she's witnessing our children's joy. For me, that's the primary focus of unschooling: helping our children live as joyfully as possible. Everything else will naturally follow from that. As long as our children are happy, they will have confidence in themselves that they can achieve anything they want to in life. I truly believe that, and unschooling is the better vehicle toward living joyfully than any schooling-based alternative.

One final note—I've continued my study of childhood education and discovered last year a scholarly work by evolutionary psychologist Peter Gray of Boston College. His book *Free to Learn* argued quite convincingly using our evolution as a species, anthropology, and his experiences with the Sudbury Valley schooling model (based on the unschooling philosophy of total educational freedom) that play is the vehicle through which human beings learn best. This has given me added confidence that my family is on the right path toward a peaceful, joyful, and prosperous future.

Skyler Collins lives with his beautiful wife and three wonderful children in Salt Lake City, Utah. He enjoys reading, writing, and podcasting about anything on liberty, economics, philosophy, religion, science, health, and childhood development. He and his wife are committed to raising their children in peace and love, exploring the world with them, and showing them how to deal with others respectfully, and enjoy their freedom responsibly. He can be found online at Facebook.com/skylerjcollins.

4 SENIOR UNSCHOOLING DADS

David Friedman
Law Professor, California, USA

Editor's Note: The following was originally written in 2007. It was submitted by the author with an updated postscript at the end.

I've decided to write on how we educate our children in two parts. The first part will describe the arguments for our approach, and the second our experiences with it.

Theory

Our approach starts with the fact that I went to a good private school, my wife to a good suburban public school, and both of us remember being bored most of the time; while we learned some things in school, large parts of our education occurred elsewhere, from books, parents, friends, and projects. It continues with some observations about the standard model of K-12 schooling, public and private:

1. That model implicitly assumes that, out of the enormous body of human knowledge, there is some subset that everyone should study and that is large enough to fill most of thirteen years of schooling. That assumption is clearly false. Being able to read and do arithmetic is important for almost everyone. Beyond that, it is hard to think of any particular subject which there is a good reason for everyone to study, and easy to think of many subjects outside the standard curriculum which there are good reasons for some people to study.

2. It also implicitly assumes that the main way in which one should learn is by having someone else tell you what you are going to study this week, what you should learn about it, and your then doing so.

As some evidence of the failure of that model, consider my wife's experience teaching a geology lab for non-majors at Virginia Polytechnic Institute, probably the second best public university in the state. A large minority of the students did not know that the volume of a rectangular solid—a hypothetical ore body—was the length times the height times the depth. Given that they were at VPI they must have mostly been from the top quarter or so of high school graduates in Virginia; I expect practically all of them had spent at least a year each studying algebra and geometry.

As all students and most teachers know, the usual result of making someone study something of no interest to him is that he memorizes as much as he has to in order to pass the course, then forgets it as rapidly as possible thereafter. The flip side of that, routinely observed by parents, is that children can put enormous energy and attention into learning something that really interests them—the rules of Dungeons & Dragons, the details of a TV series, the batting averages of the top players of the past decade.

Quite a long time ago, we got our kids Gameboys with Pokemon cartridges; at about the same time I heard a lady on talk radio explaining that kids who got high tech toys played with them for half an hour or so and then put them on the shelf. My estimate is that my two children logged something like eighty hours a month, perhaps more, on those cartridges for many months thereafter—more work and more attention than I, at a similar age, put into all of my schoolwork combined—and continued to play the game at a reduced rate for years thereafter. The skill they were learning, how to find their way around a world and accomplish goals therein, was in one sense useless, since the world was a fictional one. But being able to find one's way around a new environment and accomplish things within it is a very useful real world skill.

3. A related assumption is that you learn about a subject by having someone else decide what is true and then feed it to you. That is a very dangerous policy in the real world and not entirely safe even in school—many of us remember examples of false information presented to us by teachers or textbooks as true. A better policy is to go out looking for information and assembling it yourself.

Part of what that requires is the skill of judging sources of information on internal evidence. Does this author sound as though he is making an honest attempt to describe the arguments for and against his views, the evidence and its limits, or is he trying to snow the reader? That is a skill that is taught in the process of learning things for yourself, especially online. It is anti-taught by the standard model of K-12 education, in which the student is presented with two authorities, the teacher and the textbook and, unless the teacher is an unusually good one, instructed to believe what they tell him.

We concluded that the proper approach for our children was unschooling, which I like to describe as throwing books at them and seeing which ones stick. Leave them free to learn what they want, while providing suggestions—which they are free to ignore—and support. Put them in an environment—web access, people to talk with, visits to the library—that offers many alternatives. If, at some future point, they discover that they need something that was left out of their education, they can learn it then—a more efficient strategy than trying to learn everything they might ever find useful, most of which they won't.

Practice

When our daughter was five, she was going to a local Montessori school. Her mother thought she was ready to learn to read; they didn't. So Betty taught her to read, using *Doctor Seuss* books. Our son, three years younger, observed the process and taught himself. We heard about the local Sudbury school, new that year, and brought our daughter over to visit. She decided she preferred it to the Montessori school, so we shifted her. A few years later we added her brother, and a few years after that we shifted to homeschooling.

The Sudbury model includes classes if students want them. When our daughter was about ten there was a class, lasting somewhat over a year, in math. It started by assuming the students knew nothing and ended with the early stages of algebra. That is pretty much all of the formal instruction either of them had. In addition, we required them to learn the multiplication tables, which are useful to know but boring to learn. That, I think, was the closest thing to compulsory learning in their education.

How did they get educated? They both read a lot, and although some of the books they read were children's books, pretty early they were also reading books intended for adults. When our daughter was about nine we were traveling and ran out of books for her to read, so she read the Elizabeth Peters books her mother had brought along—and liked them. A few years later our son, about eight, went everywhere carrying the big one volume edition of *The Lord of the Rings*.

Betty remembered having liked and learned from *How To Lie With Statistics*—actually about how not to be fooled by statistical arguments—so we got a copy and both kids liked it. Our son likes D&D and other games with dice rolling, so he was interested In learning how to figure out the probability of getting various results. It turned out that the same author and illustrator had produced a book on simple probability theory—*How to Take a Chance*—so we got it and he read it multiple times. The result was a ten year old (I'm guessing—we didn't keep records) who could calculate the probability of rolling 6 or under with three six-sided dice. For the last few years his hobby has been creating games. At the Los Angeles World Science Fiction Convention he had an interesting and productive conversation with Steve Jackson of Steve Jackson Games concerning a game my son had invented; currently one of his ambitions is to get a board game commercially published by age sixteen.

I am fond of evolutionary biology, and so I recommended *The Selfish Gene* to my daughter. She liked it, found the approach intriguing, and read other things. Currently she is waiting for me to finish *The Moral Animal* so that we can discuss it. She also likes economics. At this point she has audited four of the classes I teach at the law school, following them at the level of the better students. She also has her own footnote in one of my articles, crediting her with a significant point she contributed to it.

Both kids spend a lot of time online. We discovered that Bill had taught himself to type when the family was playing a networked game on the home network—Diablo or Diablo II—and misspelled words started appearing on our screen. He needed to type because he played games online and wanted to be able to communicate. Later he wanted to learn how to spell so that he wouldn't look stupid to the people he was communicating with. His sister spends a good deal of time on World of Warcraft, some of it writing up battle reports and other essays to be posted on suitable web sites. She too wants her writing to look good and so consults, usually with her mother, on how best to say things.

I am fond of poetry and know quite a lot of it. When our daughter was little, I used it to put her to sleep. Sometime thereafter we were driving somewhere at night and heard a small voice from the back seat reciting "Lars Porsena of Clusium, by the nine gods he swore"—the opening lines of "Horatius at the Bridge"—in a two-year-old's lisp. She now knows quite a lot more poetry. When I put my son to bed—my wife and I take turns—we generally talk for a while, then he asks for some poems.

A few years back, I read and recommended to my daughter Duff Cooper's excellent biography of Talleyrand. She noticed the references to Talleyrand's memoirs and decided that, since some of her writing involved politics, it would be interesting to learn about it from a world class practitioner. I found her an English translation; she is now part way through the first volume.

Some years ago our daughter decided she was seriously interested in music. Since then she has participated regularly in two choirs—one at her mother's church, one specializing in early music—and taken harp lessons. She practices because she wants to, not because we make her. She is thinking of majoring in music in college, then trying to get a job as an editor. As some evidence of her qualifications, she has edited some of my manuscripts and done a useful job. Our current plan is for her to do some volunteer proofreading for the firm that published my novel.

But the largest part of their education, after reading, is probably conversation. We talk at meals. We talk when putting one or the other of them to bed. My daughter and I go for long walks at night and spend them discussing the novel I'm writing or the characters she role-plays on World of Warcraft.

Our most recent concern has been getting our daughter, now 17, into college. She doesn't have grades and she doesn't have a list of courses taken. She does have a list of books read—still incomplete, but already in the hundreds.

Without grades she needed another way of convincing colleges of her ability, and standardized tests were the obvious solution. She spent some time studying for the SAT exams, but enormously less than the time she would have put in on those subjects in any conventional school, did extremely well on the verbal, tolerably on the math; her combined score is well within the range for the students at the very selective liberal arts colleges she plans to apply to. Just to play safe she has now taken the SAT exams again, after spending a little more time on math, part of it solving pages of simple equations I produced for her. To keep it interesting, I included a few that no value of X

solved, a few that all values of X solved, and a few that reduced to 1/x=0.

Many schools now require two of the SAT II achievement tests—again especially significant for a homeschooled student. It turns out that "literature" is not, as I feared, a test of what you have read but of how well you can read, and she reads very well. For a second one she chose American history, read all of Paul Johnson's *A History of the American People*—well written and opinionated, hence not boring—plus part of a book of primary source material. She spent a good deal of time in the week before the exam using Wikipedia to compile her own timeline of Presidents and what happened during their terms. The results of both exams were satisfactory.

What is the result? Our daughter will enter college knowing much more about economics, evolutionary biology, music, renaissance dance, and how to write than most of her fellow students, probably less about physics, biology, and world history, except where it intersects historical novels she has read or subjects that interest her. She will know much more than most of them about how to educate herself. And why.

Postscript

Our daughter spent two years at Oberlin, transferred to the University of Chicago, and ended up majoring in Italian, another of her interests. Along the way she translated, and I webbed, a 15th century Italian cookbook.[18] She is now back with us, developing a career as an online freelance editor. Her brother spent three years at Chicago majoring in history, took last year off to see if he could write a publishable novel. He has written a (very odd) novel which we think is publishable and plan to send to my agent as soon as his sister finishes one more editorial pass on it. If we are right, we see no particular reason why he should go back for a final year of school, but that will be up to him.

David Friedman is an economist and legal scholar with a doctorate in physics. He currently teaches at the Santa Clara University School of Law. He is a widely published scholar with more than three decades of experience in academia, having taught extensively at both the undergraduate and graduate levels. He can be found online at Facebook.com/david.friedman.948011.

---

[18] View online at http://skyler.link/dfduelibreb

ON THEIR UNCONVENTIONAL APPROACH TO EDUCATION

Mike Durland
Entrepreneur, North Carolina, USA

Editor's Note: The following is a lightly edited version of an audio recording submitted for this book.

My son went to public school for five years. I didn't understand for a long time the damage it was doing. When I grew up I went to public school for the majority of the time; there were a couple of times I went to private school but it was just kind of one of those things where it is just 'that's what you do.' I didn't even think about it when he was a certain age, I just thought 'time to go to school' and that's what he did. Over the years of him being in public school I noticed that he wasn't interested in any of the things that they were doing. He wasn't really learning the things that they wanted to him to learn and he was just recoiling from the whole situation, and I started to realize how damaging it could be. So I decided to take him out and get permission from the State of North Carolina to homeschool him.

Once he was home I realized that it was a bad experience at school, so he had to wait a while and I didn't want to push on things that were considered 'learning' because 'learning' in school was a very traumatic experience, so I let him have his space; I let him do his own thing and I figured ok, that is going to be a temporary thing and then we will start doing the school work later. Then I started doing some research about unschooling, doing your own thing, and since you are highly motivated in what you are doing, you are actually learning a whole lot doing your own thing. Playing and experimenting and exploring and doing things like that. So back then I was selling and repairing used appliances I was travelling around and he would go with me everywhere I went basically. He saw me negotiate with customers, he was experiencing that, he was experiencing the whole selling and buying and the work involved with everything and how much effort it took me to make money. That was another thing that when he was real young he took care of his own finances, so he was able to experiment with money and buy and sell things at flea markets and different places and he would have money and then he would spend it, and then he would sometimes regret it, sometimes he was happy and sometimes he would resell things that he had bought and would maintain a certain pool of money. He was learning a lot of negotiating skills and the value of money and having money and having his own property with the money. That was his and he could do what he wanted with it. I think that was a really good thing and I think that is something that should be taught to children that as soon as they are able to count they have their own money and they have some kind of control over their own finances almost immediately because it takes a long time to grow those skills.

So now he is 19 and an only child, we are not going to have any more; my own parents were on and off, breaking up, getting back together, they moved around all over the country, so I went to twenty-seven different schools. As soon as I went to one school and got a little bit settled we were moving again and stuff like that. All the changing scenery and all the different people I got to know didn't really make me realize the slow grind of staying in the same school for so long. Looking back I guess that was a positive thing that I wasn't completely deteriorated as far as my character in public school because I was able to move around and meet different people and everything was more fresh and new so the school experience, at least at that time, didn't seem as bad. There were sometimes it was but it was new and, you know, when you are new to a school people give you the benefit of the doubt and they are not so hard on you, they are a little bit nicer to you. Those were all positives.

When I first took Jacey out of public school I got a lot of pushback from other people. They thought it was a bad idea, they didn't understand, they just thought I had to go and complain to the school and stuff like that, but I was just really going with my gut at the time because I hadn't really done any research or anything like that, this was a while ago and I didn't have fast Internet and that kind of stuff so I was more going with my gut. If I were to go back in time and reassure myself I would say that that is the best decision, because for one thing just getting out of the public school is such a positive part of the whole process. What you do after is just icing on the cake as far as what a child learns and things like that. So just getting out of the negative is such a huge positive. That is the main thing, number one that you have to understand is that public school is a forced situation and it literally grinds down the character. The child must adapt to the psychotic environment and they have to push themselves down. They have to shrink themselves. They have to chip off their own personality to match the insane environment knows as public school. So just not being in that situation, just that is such a great positive. That right there in itself, if the child remains illiterate the rest of his life—that is what a lot of people think, if you aren't in school you are not going to learn anything and that is just completely ridiculous, but let's just say that was true—then at least they can be themselves besides conforming to an insane environment.

Of course learning how to read is nothing; learning math skills, learning negotiation skills, learning all of these skills that are actually important in your life in their context. Learning math on a timed test or learning math on a worksheet is not in any productive context. It's just busy work. Something that is just arbitrarily put onto you as a child and you don't understand what the purpose is. There is no purpose in that moment. When you are actually trying to figure something out because you are trying to accomplish something, then the math skills and the reading skills and the history skills and whatever skill it is that you need to accomplish what you want to accomplish, literally your brain can wrap around just about anything so rapidly and in a fulfilling manner because it is something that you want to do. So you have this momentum of desire that ploughs you right through all the learning hurdles.

All those things just started happening and I was just kind of passive in the whole unschooling thing, not passive but not really like "Hey sit down, it's time for schoolwork," and stuff like that, or this is what we are going to do now. That didn't really happen and I realized that if I just get out of the way, then learning is accomplished through his desires on what he wants to do. It was just like an amazing transformation from really recoiling and not having any desire to learn because of such a negative situation in school, and then slowly transforming into—wait a minute—*loving* learning and *wanting* to learn everything possible to be a better person, to have a better life and to be positive and productive toward other people. That is the whole unschooling thing in a nutshell. A quick, easy explanation of how I experienced it; it wasn't through reading books and going through a methodology, it was just like escaping a traumatic situation and then realizing that this is a much better situation; this is going to work way better than going to public school for sure. Yes, I did have some doubts in the beginning; I thought "Maybe this isn't the right thing," but I went with my gut as I was seeing a negative situation, and responding to that. I was reacting to the negative situation. For somebody who is actually considering this in advance, going into it with some understanding, it will be the absolute best thing you can do for your children, yourself, your family and everyone around you. In the end this is the direction that people are going. It's crazy to me that public schools still exist now that I have experienced this better way, but that is from my perspective. I think eventually it's just going to phase out, hopefully anyway, as soon as possible.

Those are my main points there as far as the whole transition process. Do the right thing. Don't worry about it. Your kids will amaze you, and just being there as a facilitator, you will start learning more yourself, actually.

One of the biggest concerns that a lot of people have, I think, is college. They have this mindset that you have to go to high school and get good grades in high school so that you can have SAT scores, and so you can have a diploma and all of that stuff in order to get into a good college; and why do you need to get into a good college? So that you can get a good job and stuff like that. There are lots of studies that show that people that graduate college make more money and stuff like that but there is also a lot of opportunity costs there to factor in that a lot of people don't factor in. Besides that point, my son Jacey is here, he is 19 and I wanted him to explain what he plans on doing with his future, so you can just get an idea of what a person can do in a situation of unschooling for the majority of his life. He went to public school for five years, and there was a transition time of trying to recoup from that.

Jacey, what do you plan on doing? Do you plan on going to college anytime in the future?

"Since I wasn't forced to go to high school it gave me the luxury to go ahead and work on my skills and my life goals then. So now I am already pretty adept at the skills that I have that I need to fulfill my life goals. I have my goals, I have them figured out, I know what I want to do as far as a career goes and I would not go to college because they are just not compatible to what my goals are, what I want to do, what I want my career to be. I don't think they can in any way efficiently improve the skills that I need and the mindset that I need to fulfill my goals."

Your goals require a lot of skills so this is something that it would take forever in college to learn how to do right?

"Yes."

And are you planning on sending any of your kids to public school?

"Never, any school. Never."

Ok so there you have it. Those are the main things and thoughts on the subject. It is kind of a personal thing and everyone is in different situations, so it is kind of one of those things that if we can throw out some information, then hopefully it is useful to somebody, and of course we will be glad to talk to anybody who would even consider taking their kids out of public school, much less unschooling or homeschooling, or whatever.

Mike Durland is an entrepreneur and has been for most of his life. He runs a YouTube channel doing car reviews. He can be found online at Facebook.com/mike.durland.7.

Peter Gray
Psychology Professor, Massachusetts, USA

Editor's Note: The following was originally published as the Prologue in the author's book, Free to Learn.[19] It was submitted by the author.

"Go to hell!" The words hit me hard. I had on occasion been damned to hell before, but never so seriously. A colleague, frustrated by my thickheaded lack of agreement with an obvious truth, or a friend, responding to some idiotic thing I had said. But in those cases "go to hell" was just a way to break the tension, to end an argument that was going nowhere. This time it was serious. This time I felt, maybe, I really would go to hell. Not the afterlife hell of fire and brimstone, which I don't believe in, but the hell that can accompany life in this world when you are burned by the knowledge that you have failed someone you love, who needs you, who depends on you.

The words were spoken by my nine-year-old son, Scott, in the principal's office of the public elementary school. They were addressed not only

---

[19] Available in several formats at http://skyler.link/amznfree2learn

to me but to all seven of us big, smart adults who were lined up against him—the principal, Scott's two classroom teachers, the school's guidance counselor, a child psychologist who worked for the school system, his mother (my late wife), and me. We were there to present a united front, to tell Scott in no uncertain terms that he must attend school and must do there whatever he was told by his teachers to do. We each sternly said our piece, and then Scott, looking squarely at us all, said the words that stopped me in my tracks.

I immediately began to cry. I knew at that instant that I had to be on Scott's side, not against him. I looked through my tears to my wife and saw that she, too, was crying, and through her tears I could see that she was thinking and feeling exactly as I was. We both knew then that we had to do what Scott had long wanted us to do—remove him not just from that school but from anything that was anything like that school. To him, school was prison, and he had done nothing to deserve imprisonment.

That meeting in the principal's office was the culmination of years of meetings and conferences at the school, at which my wife and I would hear the latest accounts of our son's misbehavior. His misbehavior was particularly disturbing to the school personnel because it was not the usual kind of naughtiness that teachers have come to expect from exuberant boys confined against their will. It was more like planned rebellion. He would systematically and deliberately behave in ways contrary to the teachers' directions. When the teacher instructed students to solve arithmetic problems in a particular way, he would invent a different way to solve them. When it came time to learn about punctuation and capital letters, he would write like the poet e.e. cummings, putting capitals and punctuation wherever he wanted to or not using them at all. When an assignment seemed pointless to him, he would say so and refuse to do it. Sometimes—and this had become increasingly frequent—he would, without permission, leave the classroom and, if not forcibly restrained, walk home. We eventually found a school for Scott that worked. A school as unlike "school" as you can imagine.

Children come into the world burning to learn and genetically programmed with extraordinary capacities for learning. They are little learning machines. Within their first four years or so they absorb an unfathomable amount of information and skills without any instruction. They learn to walk, run, jump, and climb. They learn to understand and speak the language of the culture into which they are born, and with that they learn to assert their will, argue, amuse, annoy, befriend, and ask questions. They acquire an incredible amount of knowledge about the physical and social world around them. All of this is driven by their inborn instincts and drives, their innate playfulness and curiosity. Nature does not turn off this enormous desire and capacity to learn when children turn five or six. We turn it off with our coercive system of schooling. The biggest, most enduring lesson of school is that learning is work, to be avoided when possible. My son's words in the principal's office changed the direction of my professional life as well as my personal life. I am, and was then, a professor of biopsychology, a researcher interested in the biological foundations of mammalian drives and emotions. I had been studying the roles of certain hormones in modulating fear in rats and mice, and I had recently begun looking into the brain mechanisms of maternal behavior in rats. That day in the principal's office triggered a series of events that gradually changed the focus of my research. I began to study education from a biological perspective. At first my study was motivated primarily by concern for my son. I wanted to make sure we weren't making a mistake by allowing him to follow his own educational path rather than a path dictated by professionals. But gradually, as I became convinced that Scott's self-directed education was going beautifully, my interest turned to children in general and to the human biological underpinnings of education.

What is it about our species that makes us the cultural animal? In other words, what aspects of human nature cause each new generation of human beings, everywhere, to acquire and build upon the skills, knowledge, beliefs, theories, and values of the previous generation? This question led me to examine education in settings outside of the standard school system, for example, at the remarkable non-school my son was attending. Later I looked into the growing, worldwide "unschooling" movement to understand how the children in those families become educated. I read the anthropological literature and surveyed anthropologists to learn everything I could about children's lives and learning in hunter-gatherer cultures—the kinds of cultures that characterized our species for 99 percent of our evolutionary history. I reviewed the entire body of psychological and anthropological research on children's play, and my students and I conducted new research aimed at understanding how children learn through play.

Such work led me to understand how children's strong drives to play and explore serve the function of education, not only in hunter-gatherer cultures but in our culture as well. It led to new insights concerning the environmental conditions that optimize children's abilities to educate themselves through their own playful means. It led me to see how, if we had the will, we could free children from coercive schooling and provide learning centers that would maximize their ability to educate themselves without depriving them of the rightful joys of childhood.

Peter Gray is a research professor in the Department of Psychology at Boston College. The author of Psychology, *a highly regarded college textbook, he writes a popular blog called "Freedom to Learn" for* Psychology Today. *He lives in Shrewsbury, Massachusetts. He can be found online at Facebook.com/peter.gray.3572.*

Ron Patterson
Retired Major USAF, Texas, USA

I don't know a lot about unschooling. But I had faith in my wife and faith in my kids.

We have many things to learn in life but you don't necessarily have to learn any of it in school. People think that's the only way, but it's not. Frankly, I learn a lot better when someone isn't telling me what to do. I see something that crosses my path and suddenly I want to find out more about it. Then one thing leads to another... and another... and another. Why wouldn't kids be the same way?

Life is full of great adventures and you should take every opportunity to pursue them. That's how we saw it and how we lived it. Some of the things we did:

- Hiked on a volcano.
- Sailed on a tall ship in the San Francisco Bay.
- Built a horse arena.
- Built an ice rink in the back yard.
- Walked through the Red Woods (literally).
- Saw grizzly bears in the wild.
- Saw a humpback whale from about ten feet.

- Watched gray whales migrate up the coast of Alaska.
- Pitched a tent in the middle of a lake and then went ice fishing.
- Threw a cup of hot water up in the air and never saw it hit the ground (we were in Alaska).
- Participated in a civil war re-enactment on Angel Island.
- Hiked multiple mountain peaks.
- Climbed waterfalls on the banks of the Colorado River in Texas.
- Visited the deck of the only ship sunk twice in World War II (USS Enterprise).
- Learned to ride horses, raise chickens, bale hay on our own ranch.
- Learned about history, science, the world through movies together.
- Wandered around the battlefield of Custer's last stand.
- Learned about the Japanese culture as we hosted an exchange student.
- Spent a week in Washington, D.C., visiting museums, monuments, and fascinating sights.

These are some of my fondest memories – things we were able to do because we did not bother with school schedules or school ideas about what's important to learn. My kids are now grown—21, 24, and 26—all making a living, happy with their lives.

Ron Patterson has retired as a Major in the USAF and also as the Director of Christopher House, the only inpatient hospice facility in Austin, Texas. Ron leaves the online networking to his wife. She would be happy to help anyone and can be found online at Facebook.com/SuePattersonCoaching.

Terry McIntyre
Retired Computer Pro., California, USA

I'm a retired computer professional, but didn't earn much initially, back when my wife and I homeschooled; we were below or at median income until our divorce, when our two children began high school. You needn't have a six-digit income; we certainly did not. I'm also proud and delighted to be a grandfather, that my daughter has been home- or unschooling her children (seven of them from infant to 13) - and that my son is very engaged with the education of his own.

Unlike most dads, I was the initiator when it came to homeschooling. My wife had a degree in elementary education, and balked at the very idea of teaching our own. She had been trained to plan and prepare, to have formal structure, and so forth—a task which would daunt any one person. I view education completely differently, from the perspective of the student; I ask not "how to teach," but how to learn most productively. When I went to Catholic school for 11 years (skipping grade 8), I often felt that my time was being stolen from me; I wanted something better for my own—not merely in terms of "quantity of educational content," but qualitatively different.

When I started first grade, I was already somewhat adept at reading and arithmetic. The most effective way to continue to progress would have been to actually read, to play with new ideas, and interesting and challenging math problems.

This is precisely what we were not allowed to do. Instead, we spent 40 minutes or so waiting for a turn to read two lines from a *See Dick Run* book. Far better to use the same time to read interesting books at our own pace—which is what my grandchildren do. With arithmetic, we drilled and killed our way through a textbook, page by boring page. This is a horrendous waste of children's time.

My wife, the degreed educator, insisted that our son go to a "gifted" first grade class at a nice suburban school. The teacher was respected by our neighbors. We actually had to push to obtain admission for our son; the test administrators balked because his art skills, in their minds, were not quite up to snuff.

Two weeks later, our allegedly "artistically-challenged" son came home and asked, "What is 5-7?"

"What did your teacher say?"

"She says it's too complicated."

"What do you think?"

"I know that 7-5 is 2, and 7-7 is zero. So is 5-5, anything minus itself is zero. I think 5-7 must be something else, but I don't know what it is."

Anybody who can articulate all of that is ready to advance. I briefly explained the idea of negative numbers, using a thermometer diagram. I turned the diagram on its side, made it a number line, and explained how to think of negative numbers as growing to the left instead of to the right, and subtraction as moving in the opposite direction from addition. He understood immediately. I made sure he learned how to add and subtract all combinations of positive and negative numbers.

A few days later, I come home from work, he's doodling on his paper, and there's a number line. This is his own initiative, his own "work." I asked a few questions, and he had the concepts perfectly, in every particular. That took minutes, not days, weeks, or months. I never had to repeat the lesson. It stuck, because it was his question; he was interested.

My wife, observing this, had an epiphany. Our son could learn without complicated textbooks and plans and so forth—and could learn a lot more rapidly than at his "gifted" class. We began homeschooling, which continued until our children were 14 and 12 years of age. They did not have much trouble adapting to formal education. They had some gaps, but they had outstanding mathematical intuition, and rapidly mastered new material.

My wife and I chose to divide our labors. Under no circumstances was she to teach math. All the rest, she was free to do as she wished. As for math, I was (and remain) devoted to what we call "natural learning," or "organic learning," and some call "unschooling." Instead of "begin at page 1," my children and I would have random conversations—

sometimes about everyday math, sometimes about more abstract ideas such as binary arithmetic. We played many games which exercise math skills. They became skilled mental calculators, exceeding the competence of most peers.

To further illustrate the potential of organic learning, I will advance about 30 years, to a conversation with my 2nd-generation homeschooled grandson, aged 6.

I asked him to think about adding the integers from 1 to 100. The obvious but slow method is to add 1 and 2, add 3, add 4, and so on, requiring 99 additions. Or, one could write the numbers down as 1 2 3 ... 50, and write the 2nd half in reverse order, 100 99 98 ... 50, lining them up in 50 pairs. My grandson interjected "each pair adds to 101. There are 50 pairs. 5050." That was fast. Could he generalize? What is the sum of the even numbers, from 2 to 100? He pondered for a few seconds, and replied "2550" - which is correct. He was already a lightning-fast calculator. This problem stumps most high school students. At age 8 or 9, he tested at the 18th grade equivalent in math. Does he have good math genes? Yes. A prodigy? Yes, but a prodigy without a governor, who could race at his own speed. My grandchildren, as were their parents, are all very good at reading, math, and many other areas. They totally enjoy learning. At early ages, they are engaging and fearless conversationalists, expert socializers.

And that is why we teach our own. We don't want to hold them back by letting schools steal their time.

Terry McIntyre is a retired UNIX geek, software developer, and systems admin. He can be found online at Facebook.com/legalize.liberty.

Thomas Knapp
News Analyst, Florida, USA

My wife and I didn't intend to become unschoolers. From our kids' birth, we began investigating more formal homeschooling options, but both boys wanted to attend government ("public") school, and we allowed both of them to give it a try. It was a disaster.

In fairness, part of that may have been due to the particular public school system in our area, which was in complete shambles and which recently lost its accreditation and had to send all its students off to other districts.

Our oldest son loved school. He did well academically, he liked his teachers, and he was selected for the "gifted program." But over time, he frankly felt less and less physically safe. As one of only a handful of white students in a school that was almost entirely black, he found himself frequently picked on and challenged to fights. It wasn't about race *per se*. In large group situations, *any* kid who's "different" gets singled out. We switched him to an arts-oriented charter school. He enjoyed that, too, but his total commute (at ten years old, using public transit alone, by the way— free range kid!) was nearly two hours and he often received at least two hours' worth of homework. It wore him out, as his entire day consisted of school, getting to and from school, and working on school assignments.

Our younger son had discipline problems. For this, I am not going to lay the entire blame on the school, as he was and is something of a hellion. But the school does deserve part of it. I spent ten years in the Marine Corps, and that life was much less regimented than life at public school. Line up for the bathroom. No talking in line. No talking at lunch. Ten minutes of recess per day (when I was a kid, it was closer to 45 minutes split over three breaks) ... oh, and no running. And this was first grade!

So we switched to homeschooling of the sort that mimics the public school paradigm: So many hours a week "in class," a set curriculum, keeping of logs per requirements in our state (Missouri, which we've since moved away from), discrete lessons in discrete areas.

It worked out... sort of. They learned the material that we presented to them. They completed the assignments that we set them to. They did well on the tests designed to measure their progress.

But they were bored stiff, even though I tried to juggle the curriculum to match up with their interests. They resisted the regimentation ... and I didn't blame them!

Both of them were reading well before their "formal educations" began, having learned on their own with occasional help from Mom and Dad on how to sound out words and what the harder words meant.

Both of them had already achieved a basic grounding in math—arithmetic, simple algebra, a little geometry—by age 10 or so.

Both of them had a healthy interest in science and the arts.

Both of them paid attention to current events and would dig into history on their own, using Wikipedia and other online resources, to understand and intelligently discuss those events.

And the whole time, a quote from David Friedman kept coming back to mind: "We concluded that the proper approach for our children was unschooling, which I like to describe as throwing books at them and seeing which ones stick. Leave them free to learn what they want, while providing suggestions—which they are free to ignore—and support."

By the time they were 12 and 10 respectively, we had segued naturally into unschooling. The difference was dramatic and demonstrated to us that kids will learn and learn and learn... if their parents and the state will just get the hell out of the way and *let them*.

We make suggestions. We pose problems. We recommend books. We watch out of the corners of our eyes to make sure they're always doing *something*.

And they are always doing something.
They read even more on their own now than they did when we were assigning the reading.

They always have projects going—art projects, costume-for-play projects, film projects (we spent weeks on stop-motion animation), computer game coding projects—and those projects almost always present fairly advanced math problems that they either solve on their own or bring to us for assistance. They're 16 and 14 now. I don't know that they would ace a college-level trigonometry test, but they'd recognize the problems and have some idea as to how to solve those problems.

On any given day, we can count on a long discussion of science and "social studies," grounded in current events. And we're no longer surprised when one of them hits us with a fact we hadn't known ourselves concerning ancient Egypt, Napoleon's France, World War II, gender roles in the 21st century, or which company is acquiring which competitor this week.

Above and beyond "doing something," they are enjoying their teen years instead of dreading the daily trudge to the bus stop for seven hours locked up in the combination of prison and day care center that most kids call "school."

Our oldest is boning up for his GED test. We expect him to pass it easily on his first attempt and he's been checking out the class catalog from our local community college. Similarly, we think our youngest will "graduate" at 17 or 18, at least as prepared as his publicly educated peers, for life in the real world.

Is unschooling for everyone? I can't say. Perhaps some kids want or need more regimentation than unschooling usually implies. I do know that it's worked for us, if the measure of "working" is that our kids are happy, healthy, literate, numerate and socially engaged.

Thomas L. Knapp is a long-time activist. He works as director and senior news analyst at the William Lloyd Garrison Center for Libertarian Advocacy Journalism. He lives with his family in the pine woods of north central Florida. He can be found online at Facebook.com/thomaslknapp.

EPILOGUE

The editor asked, "Phil, were you going to write something for the book?"

I was. Then my brain got overpopulated. Can I keep mine short and sweet?

"I unschool because the Internet doesn't shame my kids for wrong answers. I hope this will help them never feel stress in relationship to knowledge."

You know what's funny? This feels like homework. That's how traumatized I was by school.

I am dillydallying on my good friend's book because I have no positive associations to assignments.

Anything that feels like homework shuts down my will to do that thing.

I have suffered professionally, educationally, and interpersonally because of this.

I have hurt people I deeply cared about.

Including letting down my good friend Skyler.

I am not lazy. I am not an asshole. But I hated homework. And this feels like homework. It isn't. And it's not the editor's fault. School did this to me.

That's why I unschool. I will not take the same risk with my children's future dependability.

This is embarrassing and difficult to admit.

School taught me to be passive aggressive, and it taught me that there were no real consequences to not keeping my word.

This is my biggest weakness. I am ashamed of it. But I will admit it in this book.

I mean, this would be kind of a cool epilogue, right? "The person who couldn't do the essay was Phil from the Everything-Voluntary.com podcast. Why is he being such a dick?"

And this conversation is used mostly unedited. I'm a shitty person because I still have visceral resistance to anything that even remotely resembles homework.

Tell me that wouldn't be a clincher argument against schooling? I am the reason I unschool.

- Phillip Eger, Junior Unschooling Dad

FURTHER READING

Books

Big Book of Unschooling, Sandra Dodd
Free to Learn, Pam Laricchia
Free to Live, Pam Laricchia
Free to Learn, Peter Gray
How Children Learn, John Holt
Life Learning, edited by Wendy Priesnitz
Natural Born Learners, edited by B. E. Ekoko
Parenting a Free Child, Rue Kream
Punished by Rewards, Alfie Kohn
Weapons of Mass Instruction, John Taylor Gatto

Websites

JoyfullyRejoycing.com
LifeLearningMagazine.com
LivingJoyfully.ca
NaturalChild.org/articles/learning.html
PsychologyToday.com/blog/freedom-learn
SandraDodd.com
UnschoolingSupport.com (50 Episode Podcast)

DAD INDEX

Alan Southgate *35*
Art Carden *39*
Chris Moody *11*
Danilo Cuellar *47*
David Friedman *97*
David Martin *51*
Earl Stevens *1*
Edwin Stanton *56*
Gregory Diehl *15*
Jeff Till *63*
Jeremy Henggeler *20*
John Durso *79*
Mike Durland *109*
Pace Ellsworth *82*
Parrish Miller *27*
Peter Gray *118*
Phillip Eger *137*
Rob Nielsen *86*
Ron Patterson *124*
Skyler Collins *90*
Terry McIntyre *126*
Thomas Knapp *131*

Printed in Great Britain
by Amazon